Thank you for picking up my book. Your support means a lot, and I hope you find the read both enjoyable and insightful. Beyond being an author, my work extends into research and consultancy within organizational behavior and leadership. I engage with a broad spectrum of clients, from individuals to larger teams and organizations, offering guidance in leadership development.

For a deeper dive into my professional background and consulting philosophy, several websites are available. There, you'll also find my contact details. I'm eager to hear your thoughts on the book or discuss potential collaboration in leadership coaching.

Discover more about my work and other publications related to leadership and organizational behavior at my personal website, https://thomaspatrickhuber.com.

Learn about my specific approach to leadership coaching and consulting at https://elevateus.ch, the official website of my company.

Lastly, in case you want to reach out to me directly please send me an email at thomaspatrick@mac.com.

I appreciate your support in purchasing this book and look forward to connecting with you.

Wishing you an enlightening journey,

Thomas P Huber, PhD, MS ECS

# Preface

In crafting the preface for our book, "Advanced Psychoanalytic Approach to Executive Leadership Coaching," we embark on a journey that extends beyond conventional leadership development paradigms into the rich, often uncharted territories of the human psyche. This exploration is not just an academic endeavor; it is a voyage into the depths of what it means to lead and influence with authenticity, emotional intelligence, and psychological insight.

The genesis of this book lies in the recognition that leadership, at its core, is a profoundly psychological phenomenon. The decisions leaders make, the cultures they cultivate, and the visions they articulate are all deeply rooted in psychological processes—many of which operate beyond the realm of conscious awareness. Traditional leadership development models, while valuable, often skirt the surface of these deeper dynamics. Our aim is to bridge this gap, offering a comprehensive exploration of how psychoanalytic theory—particularly the contributions of Carl Jung, Alfred Adler, Erik Erikson, Wilfred Bion, Kurt Lewin, and Manfred Kets de Vries—can illuminate the complex inner world of leaders and the organizations they shape.

This book is written for executive coaches, leadership consultants, organizational psychologists, and leaders themselves who are seeking advanced strategies for understanding and navigating the psychological underpinnings of leadership challenges. It is for those who appreciate that true leadership excellence requires not just strategic acumen and operational expertise but also a profound understanding of the self and others.

Each chapter of this book delves into the theories of one of the aforementioned psychoanalytic and psychological theorists, unraveling how their insights apply to leadership and executive coaching. From Jung's archetypes resonating within organizational cultures to Adler's notions of power dynamics, from Erikson's stages of psychosocial development influencing leader growth to Bion's group dynamics theories, Lewin's leadership styles, and Kets de Vries's examination of the psychological health of leaders and organizations, we weave a tapestry of theoretical depth and practical application.

The journey through these pages is not just an intellectual exercise but an invitation to a deeper mode of engagement with the world of leadership development. It is an invitation to consider not only how leaders act but why they act—the hidden motivations, fears, and desires that drive them. It is an invitation to explore not only the structures and strategies of organizations but also their emotional and psychological undercurrents.

As you turn these pages, I encourage you to remain open to the insights and challenges that this psychoanalytic exploration presents. The path to understanding the depths of one's own psychological landscape, and that of others, is often fraught with complexity and discomfort. Yet, it is precisely this journey into the depths that holds the promise of transformative change—change that can lead to more authentic, effective, and emotionally intelligent leadership.

In writing this book, my hope is that you, the reader, will find not only valuable theoretical insights and practical strategies for leadership development but also a deeper connection to your own inner world and the inner worlds of those you lead or coach. May this book serve as a guide on your journey toward achieving true leadership excellence, enriched by the profound insights that psychoanalytic theory offers.

# Introduction

In the dynamic and often tumultuous landscape of 21st-century leadership, the call for leaders who are not only strategic visionaries but also emotionally intelligent and psychologically aware has never been louder. The challenges facing today's leaders—ranging from navigating digital transformations to leading diverse and geographically dispersed teams—demand a depth of understanding and insight that traditional leadership models often fail to provide. It is within this context that the exploration of advanced psychoanalytic concepts in leadership coaching becomes not just relevant but essential.

This book is born out of the recognition that the complexities of modern leadership cannot be fully addressed through surface-level interventions or by focusing solely on behaviors and skills. Instead, there is a profound need for leaders to engage with the deeper psychological processes that influence their thoughts, feelings, and actions. Advanced psychoanalytic concepts offer a lens through which these processes can be examined, understood, and, ultimately, navigated with greater awareness and efficacy.

Psychoanalysis, with its rich exploration of the unconscious mind, provides invaluable insights into the motivations, fears, and desires that drive human behavior. When applied to leadership coaching, these insights have the power to transform not only individual leaders but also the cultures and organizations they lead. By delving into the depths of psychoanalytic theory, leaders can embark on a journey of self-discovery that reveals the hidden drivers behind their leadership styles, decision-making processes, and interpersonal dynamics.

The rationale for this exploration is clear: as the demands on leaders continue to evolve, so too must our approaches to leadership development. The aim of this book is to bridge the gap between traditional leadership coaching methods and the profound insights offered by psychoanalytic theory. In doing so, we hope to equip leaders and coaches with the tools they need to navigate the complexities of leadership in the 21st century with greater depth, authenticity, and emotional intelligence.

As we venture into the realm of advanced psychoanalytic concepts, we invite readers to approach this exploration with an open mind and a willingness to engage with the often challenging yet deeply rewarding process of psychological inquiry. The journey ahead promises to be one of transformation, offering new perspectives on leadership and the potential for profound personal and professional growth.

Today's leaders navigate an unprecedented array of challenges that extend far beyond the traditional boundaries of organizational management and strategic implementation. The rapid pace of technological innovation, the complexities of global interconnectedness, and the increasing emphasis on diversity and inclusion are but a few of the multifaceted issues that demand a new kind of leadership acumen. Moreover, the psychological toll of leading through periods of uncertainty—such as those brought on by global pandemics, economic volatility, and social upheaval—calls for a depth of understanding and resilience that cannot be cultivated through conventional leadership training alone.

The necessity for deeper psychological insight becomes apparent as leaders are required to manage not just the operational and strategic aspects of their roles but also the human, emotional, and psychological dimensions. Today's leaders must be adept at navigating their own internal landscapes as well as understanding and influencing the complex psychological dynamics of their teams and organizations. This includes fostering a culture of psychological safety, managing team dynamics under stress, and supporting the well-being of employees while driving performance and innovation.

Leaders are also confronted with the challenge of authenticity in a world where stakeholders demand transparency and ethical accountability. The journey to authentic leadership is inherently a psychological one, involving deep self-reflection, the confrontation of personal fears and insecurities, and the ongoing development of emotional intelligence. Authentic leaders are those who have explored their own motivations, values, and behaviors at a profound level and have aligned their leadership practices with their inner truths.

The role of a leader as a catalyst for change within organizations has never been more critical. Leading change requires more than just strategic vision; it requires an understanding of the human resistance to change, the ability to inspire and mobilize individuals at an emotional level, and the capacity to navigate the anxieties and uncertainties that invariably accompany transformational efforts. Psychoanalytic concepts offer invaluable tools for understanding these deeply human aspects of organizational change and for developing strategies to address them effectively.

In light of these challenges, the necessity for leaders to possess a deeper psychological insight is evident. Such insight enables leaders to better understand themselves and others, to manage complex interpersonal dynamics with empathy and clarity, and to lead with a sense of purpose and authenticity. It is through this deeper exploration of the self and the psychological underpinnings of human behavior that leaders can truly rise to the demands of the 21st century, transforming challenges into opportunities for growth, innovation, and meaningful impact.

**The Psychoanalytic Perspective**

Psychoanalysis, as a discipline, was pioneered in the late 19th and early 20th centuries by Sigmund Freud, whose revolutionary ideas about the unconscious mind, dreams, and the dynamics of personality development laid the groundwork for a new understanding of human behavior and mental processes. Freud introduced concepts such as the id, ego, and superego to describe the forces that drive human actions and the conflicts that arise within the psyche. His work on defense mechanisms, such as repression and projection, offered insights into how individuals protect themselves from psychological distress.

From these beginnings, psychoanalysis has evolved significantly, branching into various schools of thought that have expanded upon, diverged from, and sometimes challenged Freud's original theories. This evolution has seen the incorporation of broader psychological insights, reflecting contributions from figures such as Carl Jung, who introduced the concepts of the collective unconscious and archetypes, and Alfred Adler, known for his emphasis on social interest and feelings of inferiority and superiority as driving forces in human behavior.

The discipline has also been enriched by the work of later theorists like Melanie Klein, who focused on early childhood development and object relations, and Donald Winnicott, whose studies on the true self and false self further nuanced our understanding of human identity and emotional development. These contributions, among others, have led to a more complex and multifaceted view of psychoanalysis, one that encompasses a wide range of human experiences and psychological phenomena.

Psychoanalysis today is a diverse field that not only delves into the depths of individual psychology but also examines the ways in which unconscious processes manifest in culture, art, and societal structures. It continues to be a vital source of insights for understanding the human condition, influencing areas ranging from literature and film to therapy and, crucially, leadership development.

The evolution of psychoanalysis from its origins with Freud to its current state reflects a discipline that is both rooted in deep historical foundations and dynamically engaged with the ongoing exploration of human psychology. Its broadened scope and the diversity of perspectives within psychoanalytic thought provide a rich framework for examining the complexities of leadership in the modern world, offering leaders and executive coaches profound tools for insight, growth, and transformation.

At the heart of effective leadership lies a complex web of psychological processes, many of which unfold beyond the realm of conscious awareness. This intricate interplay between the visible and the hidden aspects of leadership underscores the notion that to lead others effectively, one must first navigate the depths of one's own psyche. Leadership is not merely a function of cognitive skills or strategic acumen; it is profoundly shaped by emotions, unconscious motivations, and deeply ingrained patterns of thought and behavior.

The unconscious mind, a concept brought to the forefront of psychological thought by the pioneers of psychoanalysis, plays a crucial role in shaping leadership styles and behaviors. It stores our deepest fears, desires, and conflicts, many of which stem from early life experiences. These hidden drivers can influence how leaders perceive challenges, make decisions, and interact with their teams. For instance, a leader's approach to risk and innovation may be unconsciously tempered by a fear of failure rooted in past experiences, while their manner of communicating and relating to others may reflect deeper needs for approval or recognition.

Leadership involves navigating not only one's own psychological complexities but also those of the individuals and groups one leads. The dynamics of power, authority, and influence are imbued with psychological significance, playing out through unconscious processes such as projection, transference, and countertransference. Leaders must be attuned to these dynamics, recognizing how their own unconscious biases and emotional responses can impact their relationships with team members and their overall effectiveness.

The psychological dimension of leadership also extends to the collective level, influencing organizational culture and the emotional climate of the workplace. Leaders play a key role in shaping these environments, often acting as emotional regulators for their teams. The ability to manage one's own emotional responses and to empathize with the emotional states of others is crucial in fostering a culture of trust, collaboration, and resilience.

Understanding leadership through the lens of psychoanalysis invites a deeper exploration of these unseen forces, offering insights into how leaders can develop greater self-awareness, emotional intelligence, and psychological flexibility. By engaging with the unconscious aspects of their psyche, leaders can uncover the root causes of their behaviors and attitudes, leading to more authentic and adaptive leadership practices. This process of psychological exploration and growth is not only essential for personal development but also for the cultivation of leadership that is responsive, empathetic, and effective in meeting the challenges of the modern world.

## Advancing Beyond Basics

The journey into the realm of leadership development, when enriched by psychoanalytic insights, necessitates a voyage beyond the foundational principles into more advanced territories of psychological understanding. This progression from basic to advanced psychoanalytic concepts is not merely an academic exercise; it represents a crucial step for leaders and executive coaches committed to fostering profound growth and transformation within themselves and the organizations they guide.

At the core of basic psychoanalytic principles are the explorations of the unconscious mind, the dynamics of early childhood experiences, and the mechanisms by which individuals cope with internal conflicts and external pressures. While these concepts provide invaluable insights into human behavior, advancing beyond these basics opens up a nuanced understanding of the complex psychological processes that underpin leadership and organizational dynamics.

Advanced psychoanalytic concepts delve into the intricacies of personality development, the subtleties of interpersonal and group dynamics, and the profound impact of unconscious processes on decision-making, creativity, and leadership styles. These concepts invite leaders and coaches to explore deeper layers of psychological understanding, such as the role of psychological defenses in shaping leadership behaviors, the influence of archetypal patterns on organizational culture, and the complex interplay between individual psychodynamics and collective organizational processes.

Engaging with these advanced concepts enables leaders and coaches to address the psychological underpinnings of leadership challenges more effectively. For instance, understanding the nuances of transference and countertransference can illuminate the emotional exchanges between leaders and followers, revealing how unconscious expectations and projections shape relationships and influence leadership effectiveness. Similarly, exploring the concept of the shadow can help leaders confront and integrate aspects of their personality that they have rejected or ignored, leading to greater authenticity and emotional intelligence.

Advanced psychoanalytic concepts offer powerful lenses through which to understand and navigate the emotional and psychological dimensions of organizational change, team dynamics, and leadership succession. They provide tools for deciphering the symbolic meanings of organizational narratives, rituals, and conflicts, allowing leaders and coaches to foster cultures of deep engagement, innovation, and resilience.

The transition to engaging with advanced psychoanalytic concepts requires a willingness to embrace complexity and ambiguity, to question deeply held assumptions, and to engage in continuous self-reflection and learning. It demands a commitment to exploring not just the light but also the shadows of leadership and organizational life, recognizing that profound growth often emerges from confronting and integrating the hidden aspects of our psyche.

For leaders and executive coaches, advancing beyond basic psychoanalytic principles to explore these deeper layers of psychological understanding is not just a path to more effective leadership; it is a journey toward a more fulfilling personal and professional life. It is an invitation to cultivate a leadership approach that is deeply informed by an understanding of the human psyche, capable of fostering transformation within individuals and organizations alike.

Advanced psychoanalytic concepts extend beyond the foundational understanding of the unconscious mind and early childhood experiences to offer nuanced perspectives on the subtleties of leadership behaviors, decision-making processes, and interpersonal dynamics. These concepts delve into the deeper strata of the psyche, providing insights into the complex interplay of psychological forces that influence leadership effectiveness and organizational health.

- Archetypal Influences and Leadership Behaviors: Carl Jung's work on archetypes introduces a framework for understanding the universal patterns of behavior that influence leaders. By recognizing how archetypal roles such as the Hero, the Sage, or the Rebel manifest in their leadership style, leaders can gain insights into their innate tendencies and motivations. This understanding allows them to adapt their behavior to better meet the needs of their organization and followers, creating a more resonant and impactful leadership presence.

- The Role of Defense Mechanisms in Decision-Making: Advanced psychoanalytic concepts also shed light on how defense mechanisms, such as denial, projection, and rationalization, influence leaders' decision-making processes. By becoming aware of these unconscious coping strategies, leaders can challenge their automatic responses and consider alternative viewpoints. This heightened self-awareness leads to more deliberate and considered decision-making, reducing the impact of biases and blind spots.

- Interpersonal Dynamics and Transference: The psychoanalytic notions of transference and countertransference provide a lens through which to examine the emotional undercurrents of leader-follower relationships. Leaders who understand how their own unresolved psychological issues may elicit certain reactions from followers—or how followers' perceptions may be colored by their own past experiences—can navigate interpersonal dynamics with greater empathy and effectiveness. This awareness facilitates the development of healthier, more productive relationships within the team or organization.

- Group Dynamics and the Unconscious: Drawing on concepts from Wilfred Bion and other psychoanalysts who have explored group dynamics, advanced psychoanalytic theory helps leaders understand the unconscious processes that influence group behavior. Knowledge of phenomena such as group regression, the basic assumption group, and the work group enables leaders to manage team anxieties, foster cohesion, and guide groups more effectively through challenges and changes.

- Emotional Intelligence and the Shadow Self: Engaging with the concept of the shadow self, or those aspects of the personality that are rejected or unseen, leaders can embark on a journey of personal integration that enhances their emotional intelligence. Recognizing and integrating the shadow not only leads to greater authenticity and self-acceptance but also equips leaders with the emotional depth to understand and respond to the emotional needs of their followers.

By engaging with these advanced psychoanalytic concepts, leaders can cultivate a leadership approach that is deeply reflective, emotionally intelligent, and psychologically informed. Such leaders are better equipped to navigate the complexities of modern organizational life, to inspire and motivate their followers, and to drive meaningful change within their organizations. The nuanced perspectives offered by advanced psychoanalytic theory empower leaders to not only understand the forces that drive their behavior but also to harness these insights for greater personal growth and organizational impact.

**Theorists and Their Contributions to Leadership**

**Carl Jung,** a Swiss psychiatrist and psychoanalyst, made seminal contributions to psychology that have profound implications for leadership and organizational culture. His concepts of archetypes and the collective unconscious introduce a rich framework for understanding the symbolic dimensions of leadership and the deep psychological currents that shape organizational life.

## Archetypes and Leadership Personas

Jung's theory of archetypes posits that there exist universal, mythic characters within the collective unconscious of people the world over. Archetypes represent fundamental human motifs of our experience as we evolved, and they evoke deep emotions. For leaders, understanding archetypes can illuminate the roles they naturally embody—such as the Hero, striving to overcome obstacles; the Sage, seeking truth and wisdom; or the Creator, driven to innovate and create. By recognizing and harnessing these archetypal energies, leaders can more effectively connect with their followers, inspire action, and guide their organizations through transformation.

## The Collective Unconscious and Organizational Culture

The collective unconscious refers to structures of the unconscious mind which are shared among beings of the same species. In the context of an organization, this concept helps explain how shared beliefs, values, and norms emerge not just from explicit agreements but from deeper, often unarticulated psychological sources. Leaders who are attuned to the collective unconscious of their organization can tap into these powerful undercurrents to foster a culture that resonates with the core identities and aspirations of its members.

## Application to Leadership and Organizational Culture

Applying Jung's concepts to leadership, a leader can be seen as a symbolic figure who embodies certain archetypal qualities that either align with or challenge the prevailing culture of the organization. For example, a leader embodying the Warrior archetype in a crisis can rally the organization towards resilience and action, while a leader channeling the Caregiver archetype may foster a culture of support and nurturance during times of change.

Leaders can also use their understanding of archetypes to navigate organizational dynamics more skillfully. Recognizing the archetypal patterns at play within their teams—such as the dynamics between the Hero and the Mentor or the Rebel and the Ruler—enables leaders to cultivate a more harmonious and productive environment. By aligning their leadership persona with the needs and unconscious expectations of their followers, leaders can engender loyalty, motivate performance, and guide their organizations toward shared goals.

Jung's insights into the collective unconscious offer leaders a deeper perspective on organizational culture change. By engaging with the symbolic meanings and narratives that resonate within the collective psyche of their organization, leaders can initiate and sustain cultural transformation in a way that aligns with the deepest values and identities of its members. Carl Jung's work provides a profound and nuanced lens through which to view leadership and organizational culture. By understanding and applying the concepts of archetypes and the collective unconscious, leaders can navigate the complex psychological landscapes of their organizations with greater wisdom and effectiveness.

**Alfred Adler,** a contemporary of Freud and Jung, offered a unique perspective on individual psychology that has significant implications for leadership, particularly in the realms of power dynamics and the role of social interest. Adler viewed power not simply as a means of dominance or control but as a manifestation of the individual's striving for significance and success within a community. This view shifts the focus from power over others to power with others, emphasizing cooperation and contribution to the collective well-being.

Central to Adler's theory is the concept of social interest, or Gemeinschaftsgefühl, which he considered a fundamental criterion for mental health and a key driver of human motivation. In the context of leadership, social interest translates to a leader's capacity to act with a deep sense of empathy, concern, and commitment to the group or community they are part of. Adler believed that true leadership is not about advancing one's own position or agenda but about contributing to the success and happiness of others.

Adler's insights into power dynamics underscore the importance of understanding leadership as a relational and ethical practice. Leaders who embody Adlerian principles prioritize the development of a cooperative environment where power is used to uplift, mentor, and mobilize towards common goals rather than to segregate, dominate, or intimidate. This approach fosters a culture of mutual respect, where the contributions of each member are valued, and the collective goals of the organization are pursued with a shared sense of purpose.

Adler's emphasis on social interest challenges leaders to look beyond the confines of their organizations and consider their broader impact on society. It encourages leaders to envision their roles in terms of societal contribution and to leverage their influence for social good. This broader perspective on leadership resonates with contemporary movements towards corporate social responsibility and ethical leadership, highlighting the relevance of Adler's work in today's leadership discourse.

Adler's contributions to our understanding of power dynamics and social interest in leadership offer a blueprint for leaders who aspire to create positive change within their organizations and communities. By embracing Adlerian principles, leaders can cultivate environments where power is exercised with responsibility and integrity, and where leadership is an expression of a profound commitment to the welfare of others.

**Erik Erikson's** theory of psychosocial development provides a nuanced framework for understanding the evolution of leadership qualities and the challenges leaders face at various points in their lives. From infancy through late adulthood, each stage of development poses a unique conflict, the resolution of which shapes an individual's capacity for empathy, effective decision-making, and resilience.

In infancy, the challenge of trust versus mistrust lays the groundwork for future leaders to develop secure relationships and dependability, essential for fostering team cohesion and collaboration. As leaders move into early childhood, grappling with autonomy versus shame and doubt, they cultivate a sense of personal control and independence, critical for confident decision-making and encouraging team autonomy.

The preschool years bring the conflict of initiative versus guilt, where the ability to take risks and innovate without being paralyzed by guilt is developed. This stage is pivotal for leaders to drive creativity and action within their organizations. During the school age period, the focus shifts to industry versus inferiority, where leaders build competency, diligence, and a strong work ethic, laying the foundation for achieving goals and setting high standards for their teams.

Adolescence is marked by the challenge of identity versus role confusion, a stage where leaders solidify their values, beliefs, and leadership style. This clarity is essential for authentic leadership and effective guidance. Young adulthood introduces the conflict of intimacy versus isolation, emphasizing the importance of forming deep, meaningful connections. For leaders, mastering this stage enhances their relationships with followers and strengthens team dynamics.

In middle adulthood, the concept of generativity versus stagnation comes to the fore, highlighting the leader's focus on mentoring, legacy building, and making lasting contributions. This altruistic approach to leadership ensures that their impact endures beyond their tenure. Lastly, late adulthood presents the conflict of ego integrity versus despair, where leaders reflect on their life and leadership journey, seeking to impart wisdom and guide future generations.

Through Erikson's stages of psychosocial development, we gain insight into the psychological underpinnings of effective leadership across the lifespan. By reflecting on their own journey through these stages, leaders can identify areas of strength and potential growth, addressing challenges with a deeper understanding of their psychological origins. Additionally, this framework allows leaders to better support the developmental needs of their team members, fostering an environment of growth and understanding within their organizations.

**Wilfred Bion's** contributions to the field of psychoanalysis extend into the understanding of group dynamics, offering profound insights into how teams and organizations behave. At the heart of Bion's theory is the concept that groups operate under two distinct modes: the work group and the basic assumption group. The work group is focused on the task at hand, driven by shared goals and rational thinking. In contrast, the basic assumption group falls under one of three unconscious assumptions—dependency, fight-flight, or pairing—each of which dictates the group's behavior based on primal, instinctive needs rather than the task.

Bion's exploration into the basic assumption group reveals how groups can regress to a more primitive state of functioning when under stress or uncertainty. For instance, a group operating under the dependency assumption looks to a leader to provide security and direction, much like a child depends on a parent. Under the fight-flight assumption, the group may band together against a perceived threat or disperse in avoidance. The pairing assumption has the group focusing on two members whose anticipated union is fantasized to resolve the group's problems.

The implications of Bion's theory for understanding team and organizational behavior are significant. It highlights the importance of recognizing when a group shifts from a work-oriented to a basic assumption mode, which can hinder productivity and rational decision-making. Leaders, by understanding these dynamics, can develop strategies to guide their teams back to a work group orientation, addressing the underlying anxieties and redirecting focus towards common objectives.

Bion's insights into group dynamics emphasize the role of emotional experiences within teams and organizations. The unconscious processes that influence group behavior can impact everything from team cohesion and conflict resolution to leadership effectiveness and organizational culture. By applying Bion's theory, leaders can better navigate the complex emotional undercurrents of their teams, fostering environments where rationality and task orientation prevail, while also addressing the psychological needs that drive basic assumption behaviors. Wilfred Bion's theory on group dynamics provides a critical framework for understanding the often-unconscious processes that influence team and organizational behavior. By recognizing and managing these dynamics, leaders can promote healthier, more productive group interactions and steer their organizations towards achieving their collective goals.

**Kurt Lewin's** pioneering research in the fields of leadership styles and group dynamics has left an indelible mark on the understanding of organizational behavior, with its roots deeply embedded in psychoanalytic thought. Lewin, often regarded as the father of social psychology, introduced the concepts of autocratic, democratic, and laissez-faire leadership styles, each characterized by distinct approaches to decision-making, authority, and team interaction. His work elucidated how these styles impact group cohesion, motivation, and productivity, offering early empirical evidence of the psychological underpinnings of leadership effectiveness.

At the heart of Lewin's theory was the notion that the behavior of individuals within groups is not merely a product of their personality traits but is significantly influenced by the dynamics of the group itself. This perspective reflects a psychoanalytic influence in its acknowledgment of the unconscious factors—such as shared anxieties, desires, and conflicts—that shape group behavior. Lewin's force field analysis further underscored this point, presenting a method to map the complex forces, both driving and restraining, that affect group change. This model, grounded in the idea that human behavior is the result of tensions between opposing forces, mirrors the psychoanalytic focus on the conflict and compromise between different elements of the psyche.

Lewin's emphasis on the importance of the group environment in determining individual behavior aligns with psychoanalytic themes regarding the influence of external contexts on internal psychological states. His experimental studies, particularly those involving changes in leadership styles and their effects on group atmosphere and performance, highlight how shifts in the external environment can lead to significant changes in individual and group behavior, a concept that resonates with psychoanalytic views on the dynamic interplay between the individual and their surroundings.

Lewin's research, while not strictly psychoanalytic, was influenced by psychoanalytic ideas in its exploration of the deeper, often unconscious, processes that govern human behavior in groups. His work paved the way for subsequent theories in organizational psychology and leadership studies that continue to draw on psychoanalytic concepts to understand the complex, often hidden, forces that drive leadership and group dynamics. Acknowledging Lewin's contributions and their psychoanalytic influences provides a richer, more nuanced understanding of the psychological aspects of leadership and the behavior of individuals within groups.

**Manfred Kets de Vries** stands out as a distinctive voice in the intersection of psychoanalysis and organizational behavior, bringing to the forefront the critical importance of psychological health in leaders and their organizations. Through his extensive body of work, Kets de Vries illuminates the profound impact that emotional well-being has on leadership effectiveness and organizational success. Drawing upon psychoanalytic principles, he explores the complex inner worlds of leaders, shedding light on how their psychological makeup influences their behavior, decision-making, and ultimately, their effectiveness in leading others.

Kets de Vries's research delves into the darker aspects of leadership, such as narcissism, paranoia, and depression, demonstrating how these traits can undermine leadership effectiveness and contribute to toxic organizational cultures. By bringing these issues into the open, his work encourages a deeper understanding and dialogue around the psychological vulnerabilities leaders face. This approach not only humanizes leadership but also highlights the necessity of addressing mental health issues within the leadership development process.

Central to Kets de Vries's philosophy is the concept of the "authentizotic" organization, a workplace where authenticity and psychological well-being are prioritized, fostering environments where both leaders and employees can thrive. He posits that when leaders are emotionally healthy and self-aware, they are better equipped to create positive, productive, and innovative organizational cultures. These leaders are capable of engaging in more meaningful relationships with their followers, driving collective success while also attending to the individual growth and well-being of team members. Furthermore, Kets de Vries emphasizes the therapeutic role of executive coaching and leadership development programs in promoting emotional well-being. Through reflective practices and guided self-exploration, leaders can gain insights into their unconscious motivations, resolve internal conflicts, and develop healthier ways of relating to themselves and others. This process not only enhances their own psychological health but also has a ripple effect, improving the overall emotional climate of the organizations they lead.

By integrating psychoanalytic insights into the study of leadership and organizational behavior, Kets de Vries offers a holistic view of what it means to lead effectively. His work underscores the inextricable link between emotional well-being and leadership performance, advocating for a more compassionate and psychologically informed approach to leadership development. Through his contributions, Kets de Vries has inspired a generation of leaders and scholars to consider the deeper psychological dimensions of leadership, paving the way for more emotionally intelligent, resilient, and effective leadership practices.

**Purpose and Structure of the Book**

The primary aim of this book is to enrich the reader's comprehension of advanced psychoanalytic concepts and illuminate their practical applications within the realm of executive leadership coaching. This endeavor seeks to bridge the gap between traditional leadership methodologies and the profound insights offered by psychoanalysis, offering a more holistic approach to understanding and nurturing leadership capabilities. By delving into the nuanced theories of renowned psychoanalysts and psychologists such as Carl Jung, Alfred Adler, Erik Erikson, Wilfred Bion, Kurt Lewin, and Manfred Kets de Vries, the book provides a comprehensive exploration of the psychological underpinnings of leadership behavior, decision-making, and interpersonal dynamics.

The exploration of these concepts is not merely academic; it is aimed at providing leaders and executive coaches with practical tools and insights that can be directly applied to enhance leadership effectiveness. Through an in-depth examination of topics such as archetypes and the collective unconscious, power dynamics, stages of psychosocial development, group dynamics, and the psychological health of leaders, the book endeavors to equip its readers with the knowledge to understand the complex psychological forces at play within themselves and their organizations.

The book emphasizes the critical role of emotional well-being in leadership effectiveness, arguing that a deeper psychological insight not only fosters personal growth but also enhances the capacity to lead others with empathy, authenticity, and resilience. It highlights the transformative potential of engaging with one's own psychological landscape and the landscapes of those one leads, advocating for a leadership approach that is reflective, emotionally intelligent, and attuned to the unconscious processes that influence human behavior.

By offering a comprehensive guide to integrating advanced psychoanalytic principles into leadership coaching, this book aims to inspire a shift towards more psychologically informed leadership practices. It encourages leaders and coaches to venture beyond surface-level understandings of leadership and embrace the complexities and depths of human psychology. In doing so, it seeks to foster a new generation of leaders who are not only strategically adept but also psychologically astute, capable of navigating the challenges of modern organizational life with insight, compassion, and integrity.

This book is structured to guide readers through a deep dive into the psychoanalytic foundations of leadership, exploring the contributions of several key theorists and the practical implications of their work for leadership development. The journey begins with an introduction to the advanced psychoanalytic concepts that underpin the book's approach to executive leadership coaching, setting the stage for a detailed exploration of each theorist's contributions.

The first chapter focuses on Carl Jung, examining his theories on archetypes and the collective unconscious. It explores how these concepts apply to leadership personas and organizational culture, providing leaders with insights into the symbolic dimensions of their roles and the deep psychological currents that shape organizational life. The second chapter delves into Alfred Adler's insights into power dynamics and the importance of social interest and community feeling in leadership. It discusses how Adler's emphasis on cooperation and contribution can inform a more empathetic and effective leadership approach, emphasizing the role of leaders in fostering a sense of belonging and purpose within their teams.

Erik Erikson's stages of psychosocial development are the focus of the third chapter, highlighting how each stage influences leadership qualities such as integrity, wisdom, and generativity. This chapter offers strategies for leaders to navigate their own psychosocial development, enhancing their leadership effectiveness across their lifespan. The fourth chapter examines Wilfred Bion's theory on group dynamics, shedding light on the unconscious processes that influence team behavior and organizational culture. It discusses the practical applications of Bion's concepts for managing team anxiety, fostering effective group functioning, and navigating the emotional experiences of groups.

Kurt Lewin's research on leadership styles and group dynamics is explored in the fifth chapter, noting its psychoanalytic influences. This chapter analyzes how Lewin's leadership styles—autocratic, democratic, and laissez-faire—affect group cohesion and productivity, and how his force field analysis model can be applied to understanding and managing organizational change.

The final chapter focuses on Manfred Kets de Vries and his work on the psychological health of leaders and organizations. It emphasizes the role of emotional well-being in leadership effectiveness and discusses strategies for fostering psychological insight and emotional health among leaders and within organizations.

Each chapter not only presents the theoretical contributions of these key figures but also explores the practical implications of their work for leadership development. Through real-world examples and case studies, the book illustrates how these psychoanalytic concepts can be applied to enhance leadership practices, improve team dynamics, and foster healthier organizational cultures. By providing a comprehensive guide to integrating these advanced psychoanalytic principles into leadership coaching, the book aims to inspire a shift towards more psychologically informed leadership practices that are capable of addressing the complexities of modern organizational life.

**Significance for Leaders and Coaches**

Integrating psychoanalytic insights into leadership coaching represents a profound shift towards cultivating leadership that is not only effective but deeply authentic and emotionally intelligent. This approach, grounded in the exploration of the unconscious motivations, fears, and desires that drive human behavior, offers a pathway to understanding and harnessing the full spectrum of a leader's psychological capabilities. By delving into the depths of psychoanalytic theory, leaders and coaches can unlock a richer, more nuanced understanding of leadership dynamics, leading to transformative growth and development.

At the core of this approach is the belief that authentic leadership arises from a deep self-awareness and understanding of one's own psychological makeup. Psychoanalytic insights provide leaders with the tools to explore their inner landscapes, uncovering hidden aspects of their personalities that can influence their leadership style and effectiveness. This journey of self-discovery enables leaders to align their actions with their true selves, fostering authenticity that resonates with and inspires those around them.

The integration of psychoanalytic concepts into leadership coaching enhances emotional intelligence, a critical component of effective leadership. Emotional intelligence—the ability to understand and manage one's own emotions and to empathize with others—can be significantly deepened through psychoanalytic exploration. Leaders learn to recognize and regulate their emotional responses, understand the unconscious emotional dynamics within their teams, and navigate interpersonal relationships with greater sensitivity and insight. This heightened emotional awareness fosters a leadership style characterized by empathy, resilience, and a genuine connection with others.

The effectiveness of leadership is also amplified by this psychoanalytic approach. By understanding the unconscious processes that influence decision-making, communication, and conflict resolution, leaders can navigate the complexities of organizational life with greater clarity and purpose. Psychoanalytic insights enable leaders to address the root causes of challenges and conflicts, rather than merely managing their symptoms, leading to more sustainable and meaningful solutions. Additionally, this deeper psychological understanding equips leaders to foster a positive organizational culture, one that supports psychological well-being, encourages creativity, and aligns with the organization's values and goals. The integration of psychoanalytic insights into leadership coaching offers a powerful framework for developing leaders who are authentic, emotionally intelligent, and highly effective. This approach not only enhances the personal growth and development of leaders but also has a transformative impact on their teams and organizations. As leaders become more attuned to the psychological dimensions of leadership, they are better equipped to lead with integrity, inspire trust and loyalty, and drive organizational success. In an ever-evolving and complex world, such leadership is not just desirable; it is essential.

The engagement with one's own psychological landscape, as well as that of others, holds immense potential for both personal and professional transformation. This deep dive into the psyche, facilitated by psychoanalytic principles, offers leaders a unique opportunity to explore the undercurrents of their motivations, behaviors, and interactions. Such exploration can lead to profound changes, not just in how leaders view themselves and their roles but also in how they relate to and inspire those around them.

Personal transformation through this engagement begins with heightened self-awareness. Leaders become more attuned to their inner workings, understanding the origins of their fears, desires, and defensive mechanisms. This self-knowledge is empowering, enabling leaders to make more conscious choices about their behaviors and responses, rather than being driven by unconscious impulses. The result is a more authentic self-expression and a leadership style that is congruent with one's true self, fostering genuine connections and trust with others.

Professionally, the insights gained from exploring psychological landscapes can revolutionize leadership effectiveness. Leaders who understand the unconscious dynamics at play within their teams can navigate interpersonal relationships and team dynamics with greater skill. They become adept at recognizing and addressing not just the surface-level issues but the deeper emotional needs and conflicts that can influence team cohesion and performance. This ability to manage and leverage the emotional undercurrents within organizations leads to more adaptive, resilient, and high-performing teams.

Engaging with psychological landscapes extends beyond personal gain and team management; it can catalyze a cultural shift within organizations. Leaders who embody psychological insight and emotional intelligence set a tone that values self-awareness, empathy, and psychological safety. Such a culture encourages open communication, innovation, and shared vulnerability, creating an environment where individuals feel valued and understood. This not only enhances employee well-being and satisfaction but also drives organizational success by fostering a collaborative, innovative, and committed workforce.

The ripple effects of this transformation are far-reaching. Leaders who engage with their own and others' psychological landscapes contribute to a vision of leadership that is more humane, reflective, and effective. They inspire others to embark on their own journeys of self-discovery and growth, cultivating a generation of leaders who are equipped to face the complexities of the modern world with insight, compassion, and resilience.

The potential for personal and professional transformation through engaging with psychological landscapes is vast. It offers a pathway to leadership that is not only successful in traditional metrics but also rich in authenticity, emotional intelligence, and psychological depth. Such leadership is capable of creating meaningful change, not just within individuals and teams, but across entire organizations and, ultimately, the broader society.

**Invitation to the Reader**

As we stand at the threshold of a profound exploration into the depths of leadership and the psyche, this book invites you on a journey unlike any other—a journey into the heart of advanced psychoanalytic concepts and their application in the realm of executive leadership coaching. This expedition is not merely academic; it is a voyage of personal and professional discovery, one that promises to expand your understanding of leadership and yourself.

Embarking on this journey requires an open and reflective mindset, a willingness to dive deep into the complexities of human behavior and the unconscious forces that shape our actions and interactions. It is an invitation to look beyond the surface, to question and reflect, and to embrace the often-uncomfortable process of self-examination. The insights and knowledge you stand to gain hold the potential to transform not just your approach to leadership but your perspective on life itself.

As you navigate through the chapters, each dedicated to the contributions of thinkers like Carl Jung, Alfred Adler, Erik Erikson, Wilfred Bion, Kurt Lewin, and Manfred Kets de Vries, you are encouraged to approach their theories with curiosity and openness. Let their ideas challenge you, inspire you, and provoke deep reflection on your own leadership practice and the dynamics within your organization.

This journey is as much about discovery as it is about application. You will find that the advanced psychoanalytic concepts presented here offer practical insights for tackling the complex challenges of leadership in today's ever-evolving landscape. They provide tools for enhancing emotional intelligence, fostering authentic relationships, and creating cultures of resilience and innovation.

But beyond the practical applications, this exploration is an invitation to connect with the deeper aspects of your being—to uncover the motivations, fears, and desires that drive you and to harness these insights for greater authenticity and impact in your leadership role. It is an opportunity to learn not just how to lead others but how to lead oneself.

So, with an open heart and a reflective mind, I invite you to embark on this journey of exploration and discovery. May the pages that follow serve as a map, guiding you through the rich terrain of the psyche and the myriad ways it manifests in the realm of leadership. And may you emerge from this journey not only as a more effective leader but as a more insightful, compassionate, and integrated human being.

For leaders poised at the edge of deepening their understanding and for coaches committed to facilitating profound, lasting change, the path laid out in this exploration of advanced psychoanalytic concepts is rich with opportunities for growth, insight, and renewal.

Leaders embarking on this voyage will discover that the journey through the depths of their own psychological landscape and that of their teams can significantly enhance their effectiveness. It's a process that promises not just the acquisition of new skills but a fundamental shift in being—a transformation into leaders who are not only more adept at navigating the complexities of the modern organizational environment but who also lead with authenticity, empathy, and a profound understanding of human behavior. This is leadership that inspires, transforms, and endures.

For coaches, this journey offers a unique opportunity to deepen their practice, to move beyond the surface level of coaching interactions and touch the very core of those they guide. Armed with advanced psychoanalytic insights, coaches can facilitate a kind of change that is both deep and lasting, supporting leaders in uncovering and addressing the unconscious dynamics that influence their thoughts, feelings, and behaviors. This is coaching that goes beyond problem-solving to touch the essence of the individual, catalyzing a transformation that is holistic and pervasive.

The journey into the depths of psychoanalytic theory and its application in leadership coaching is, at its heart, a journey into the essence of what it means to lead and to facilitate change. It's a path that challenges and rewards in equal measure, offering insights that can reshape not just leadership practices but the very fabric of organizational life.

The journey you are invited to embark upon is one of discovery, challenge, and transformation. It is a journey that promises to enrich your understanding of leadership, to deepen your insights into human behavior, and to enhance your effectiveness in facilitating change. Whether you are a leader seeking to navigate the complexities of your role with greater wisdom and compassion or a coach dedicated to fostering deep, lasting growth, the exploration of these advanced psychoanalytic concepts offers a pathway to profound personal and professional transformation. May you embrace this journey with an open heart and a curious mind, ready to uncover the boundless potential that lies within.

# Chapter 1: Carl Jung and Leadership Archetypes

In the annals of psychoanalytic theory, Carl Gustav Jung stands as a towering figure whose contributions have profoundly influenced not just psychology but various facets of culture, philosophy, and indeed, leadership studies. Jung's intellectual journey began in the rich psychoanalytic tradition established by Sigmund Freud, with whom he initially shared a close collaboration. However, Jung's deepening exploration into the human psyche led him to concepts and conclusions that diverged significantly from Freudian theory, prompting a break that would mark the birth of Analytical Psychology, Jung's own psychoanalytic framework.

Jung's departure from Freud centered around fundamental disagreements over the nature of the unconscious and the drivers of human behavior. While Freud emphasized the primordial role of sexual and aggressive impulses, Jung proposed a more nuanced understanding of the unconscious, one that included both a personal dimension, shaped by individual experiences, and a collective dimension, inherited and shared among humans across cultures and epochs. This collective unconscious, as Jung termed it, is populated by archetypes—universal, mythic characters and themes that recur in art, dreams, religions, and cultural narratives, reflecting deep-seated psychological predispositions.

For Jung, these archetypes and the collective unconscious are pivotal in understanding human behavior and, by extension, leadership. He believed that leaders, like all individuals, are influenced by these archetypal patterns, which shape their motivations, behaviors, and the roles they embody within their organizations and communities. The exploration of these archetypes in the context of leadership offers profound insights into the symbolic dimensions of authority, vision, and influence.

Jung's concepts of the shadow, the persona, and the process of individuation further enrich our understanding of leadership. The shadow represents the parts of ourselves that we deny or reject, the persona is the social mask we present to the world, and individuation is the process of integrating these disparate parts into a cohesive self. For leaders, engaging with these aspects of the self is crucial for authentic leadership that resonates with depth, integrity, and wisdom.

This chapter delves into Carl Jung's seminal contributions to psychoanalytic theory and their application to leadership, with a particular focus on the role of archetypes. By exploring Jung's insights, leaders and coaches can gain a deeper appreciation of the psychological underpinnings of leadership roles and dynamics, paving the way for more authentic, effective, and transformative leadership practices.

Carl Jung's groundbreaking concepts of the collective unconscious and archetypes represent a profound shift in understanding human behavior and motivation, extending far beyond the confines of individual experiences to the very bedrock of our shared humanity. These ideas form the cornerstone of Jung's analytical psychology, offering a rich and nuanced framework for exploring the depths of the human psyche.

The collective unconscious, a term coined by Jung, refers to the part of the unconscious mind that is inherited, rather than developed from personal experience. Unlike the personal unconscious, which is composed of forgotten or suppressed memories specific to an individual, the collective unconscious is universal, shared among all humans regardless of culture or background. It is the repository of humanity's deepest psychological instincts, themes, and memories—elements that have been passed down through generations and manifest in universal symbols, myths, and archetypes.

Archetypes, as defined by Jung, are the innate, universal prototypes for ideas and may manifest in themes, symbols, dreams, and myths across cultures. These archetypes are not consciously known but inferred, emerging in art, literature, religion, and dreams, providing a common language through which our unconscious expresses itself. Key archetypes include the Shadow, representing the repressed or denied aspects of the self; the Anima and Animus, embodying the feminine and masculine aspects within us; the Hero, symbolizing bravery and the quest for achievement; and the Wise Old Man, representing knowledge and guidance.

The significance of the collective unconscious and archetypes in understanding human behavior and motivation cannot be overstated. They provide a framework for interpreting the symbolic and often irrational aspects of human life, offering insights into the universal patterns and themes that drive our thoughts, feelings, and actions. In the context of leadership, these concepts allow us to understand the deeper, often unconscious motivations of leaders and followers alike, shedding light on the symbolic roles leaders assume and the collective narratives that shape organizational cultures.

By tapping into the collective unconscious and engaging with archetypal themes, leaders can forge deeper connections with their own intrinsic motivations and with those they lead. This engagement fosters a leadership style that is resonant and authentic, capable of inspiring and mobilizing individuals towards a shared vision. Furthermore, an understanding of archetypes can help leaders navigate the complex dynamics of power, identity, and change within their organizations, enabling them to act with greater insight and empathy.

Jung's concepts of the collective unconscious and archetypes open a window into the soul of humanity, offering a profound understanding of the psychological forces that shape our lives and societies. For leaders and those dedicated to their development, these insights are invaluable tools for fostering self-awareness, motivating others, and leading with wisdom and authenticity.

**Jung's Theories on Archetypes and the Collective Unconscious**

**The collective unconscious** represents one of Carl Jung's most profound and revolutionary ideas, positing the existence of a shared psychic structure inherent in all humans. This concept extends beyond the personal experiences and memories that shape an individual's subconscious mind, reaching into a deeper, universal level of consciousness. The collective unconscious is not developed through personal experience but is a birthright, an inherited part of the human psyche, containing the accumulated experience of all humanity. It houses universal symbols, themes, and memories—archetypes that emerge across cultures and historical periods, transcending individual differences.

This shared psychic reservoir is composed of archetypes, which are primal, universal patterns and images that have existed across time and culture. These archetypes manifest in myths, dreams, literature, and art, revealing commonalities shared by humanity regardless of cultural or geographical distinctions. They are the psychic counterpart of instinct, guiding the way we perceive the world, influencing our reactions and behaviors in ways that are often outside our conscious awareness.

The collective unconscious serves as a foundation for the psychic unity of mankind. It underscores the idea that, despite the myriad differences in our individual lives and cultural backgrounds, there exists a level of our psyche that is common and universal. This shared aspect of human psychology explains why symbols and themes such as the Great Mother, the Flood, the Trickster, and the Hero's Journey appear in the myths, stories, and religions of societies separated by vast distances and time.

For leaders and those engaged in leadership development, the concept of the collective unconscious offers a powerful lens through which to understand the symbolic and emotional undercurrents that influence group and organizational dynamics. Leaders who can tap into the archetypal themes that resonate within the collective unconscious can communicate more effectively, inspire deeply, and foster a sense of shared purpose and identity within their organizations. They become adept at navigating the symbolic realm, leveraging universal narratives and symbols to mobilize collective energies and guide their teams through challenges and transformations. Moreover, the collective unconscious provides a framework for understanding the deep-rooted fears, aspirations, and motivations that drive human behavior. By recognizing these universal patterns, leaders can cultivate empathy and insight, connecting with others at a profound level and addressing the psychological needs and concerns that underlie surface behaviors and attitudes.

The collective unconscious, with its repository of universal symbols and archetypal themes, enriches our understanding of human nature and the shared psychic heritage that binds us. For those in leadership, an appreciation of this concept opens up new avenues for personal growth, enhanced relational dynamics, and the ability to lead with a sense of vision that resonates on a deeply human level.

**Archetypes,** as conceptualized by Carl Jung, are the foundational elements of the collective unconscious, serving as the instinctive patterns or images that guide human behavior, thought, and emotion across cultures and epochs. These universal motifs are not learned or acquired through personal experience; instead, they are inherent structures of the psyche, present from birth, and shared by all humanity. Their origins trace back to the earliest experiences of our ancestors, distilled over millennia into symbolic patterns that influence the way we understand and navigate the world.

The nature of archetypes is both abstract and deeply embedded in the human psyche. They are not directly observable but make their presence known through symbols, myths, dreams, and behaviors that recur across different cultures and historical periods. Archetypes themselves are psychic potentials that, when activated by personal experiences or cultural influences, take shape in the conscious mind as symbolic images or narratives. This process gives rise to universally recognizable themes such as the Hero, embarking on a journey and overcoming obstacles; the Great Mother, representing nurturance and creation; the Shadow, embodying the rejected or denied aspects of the self; and the

Anima and Animus, reflecting the feminine and masculine aspects of the psyche, respectively.

The manifestation of archetypes in human behavior is both profound and subtle. They influence the roles individuals assume, the attractions and aversions they feel, and the patterns of behavior and relationship dynamics they engage in. For example, the Hero archetype can drive an individual to take on challenges and strive for achievement, while the Shadow may manifest in behaviors stemming from unconscious fears or rejected traits. In the realm of leadership, archetypes influence not only the leader's style and approach but also the collective identity and culture of the organization.

Leaders, by understanding and engaging with archetypal patterns, can harness these powerful psychic forces to inspire and guide their teams. A leader who embodies the qualities of the Wise Old Man archetype, for example, can offer deep insight and mentorship, fostering a culture of wisdom and learning within their organization. Similarly, leaders who recognize the Shadow's presence can work towards integrating these denied or rejected aspects, leading to greater authenticity and wholeness in their leadership style.

Archetypes play a crucial role in storytelling and narrative, tools that leaders can use to communicate vision, values, and goals. By tapping into archetypal narratives, leaders can connect with the collective unconscious of their teams, mobilizing and uniting them around shared themes and objectives. This connection to universal human experiences and aspirations makes archetypal storytelling a powerful tool for inspiring action and change.

The exploration of archetypes reveals their profound impact on the tapestry of human life, offering insights into the symbolic dimensions that underpin our behaviors, relationships, and cultural expressions. For leaders and those committed to leadership development, understanding and working with archetypes opens avenues for deeper connection, more resonant communication, and transformative leadership that aligns with the deepest currents of the human psyche.

**Archetypes in Leadership**

The concept of leadership archetypes delves into the realm of symbolic images and narratives that frequently emerge in the context of leadership, drawing upon Carl Jung's theory of archetypes. These archetypal images, such as The Hero, The Wise Old Man/Woman, and The Ruler, serve as powerful templates that shape our understanding of leadership and influence the personas that leaders embody. These archetypes are not mere characters in stories but fundamental psychic patterns that resonate deeply within the collective unconscious, manifesting in the behaviors, expectations, and narratives surrounding leadership in various cultures and contexts.

The Hero archetype is perhaps the most universally recognized in the context of leadership. It represents the journey of overcoming obstacles, achieving victory against odds, and bringing about transformation. Leaders who embody the Hero archetype are seen as courageous, resilient, and driven by a sense of mission. They inspire action and change, rallying their followers to tackle challenges and pursue a shared vision. The narrative of the Heroic leader resonates deeply with our collective longing for growth, achievement, and redemption.

The Wise Old Man/Woman archetype embodies wisdom, guidance, and insight. Leaders who reflect this archetype are valued for their depth of knowledge, reflection, and ability to provide counsel. They are seen as mentors and advisors who guide their followers through complexity with a steady hand and a profound understanding of human nature and organizational dynamics. This archetype emphasizes the importance of insight, perspective, and the sharing of knowledge in leadership.

The Ruler archetype represents control, order, and authority. Leaders associated with this archetype are characterized by their strong will, decisiveness, and responsibility for maintaining structure and governance. They are often seen as the architects of systems and societies, wielding power to create stability and prosperity for their communities or organizations. The Ruler archetype underscores the aspects of leadership that relate to governance, stewardship, and the establishment of norms and standards.

Leadership archetypes influence not only how leaders perceive themselves and their roles but also how they are perceived by others. These archetypal patterns shape the expectations and dynamics within leader-follower relationships, offering a symbolic framework through which leadership is understood and enacted. By recognizing and engaging with these archetypes, leaders can tap into deeper layers of meaning and motivation, connecting with their followers on a more profound level. The conscious integration of archetypal energies can enhance a leader's effectiveness and authenticity. By reflecting on the archetypes that resonate with their personal journey and leadership style, leaders can cultivate a persona that aligns with their core values and aspirations. This alignment between the individual leader's psyche and the archetypal patterns of leadership not only enriches the leader's personal development but also fosters a more resonant and impactful leadership presence.

The exploration of leadership archetypes reveals the symbolic dimensions of leadership and the deep psychological currents that shape leaders and their narratives. Understanding these archetypal patterns provides valuable insights into the dynamics of leadership and the potential for growth, transformation, and authentic connection in the realm of leading others.

The influence of archetypes on leadership extends deeply into leadership style, communication, and decision-making processes, reflecting the profound impact these universal patterns have on the psyche of leaders and their followers. By embodying archetypal energies, leaders can shape their approach to leadership in ways that resonate on a fundamental level with those they lead, influencing not only the culture of the organization but also the effectiveness of their leadership.

Leadership Style

Archetypes directly shape a leader's style by imbuing it with qualities associated with specific archetypal patterns. A leader resonating with the Hero archetype might adopt a leadership style characterized by boldness, resilience, and a focus on overcoming challenges, often inspiring action and perseverance in the face of adversity. Conversely, a leader embodying the Wise Old Man/Woman archetype may prioritize reflection, mentorship, and the dissemination of knowledge, fostering a culture of learning and development within their team or organization. The Ruler archetype influences leaders to prioritize stability, order, and governance, emphasizing structure, control, and vision in their leadership style. Understanding these archetypal influences allows leaders to more consciously develop their unique leadership style in alignment with their intrinsic motivations and values.

Communication

Archetypal patterns profoundly influence how leaders communicate, shaping the language, symbols, and narratives they use to connect with and mobilize their followers. Leaders aligned with the Hero archetype might employ motivational and aspirational rhetoric, framing organizational goals as quests or challenges to be overcome. This type of communication can energize and rally teams, fostering a sense of shared purpose and adventure. Leaders reflecting the Wise Old Man/Woman archetype, however, might focus on storytelling and the sharing of insights, using communication as a tool for guidance and reflection. Their communication style can help create a deeper sense of understanding and connection within their teams. Ruler archetypes, in their communication, may emphasize vision, order, and the collective good, using clear, directive language to establish norms and expectations.

Decision-Making Processes

The influence of archetypes extends to the decision-making processes of leaders, affecting how they approach problems, evaluate options, and make choices. Hero-archetype leaders may approach decision-making with a focus on action and innovation, ready to take risks to achieve significant outcomes. They might favor bold moves that align with their vision of overcoming obstacles and achieving success. Leaders resonating with the Wise Old Man/Woman archetype might take a more contemplative approach to decision-making, valuing input, reflection, and the wisdom of past experiences. This can lead to more measured and thoughtful decisions that consider the long-term impact on their team and organization. Ruler-archetype leaders are likely to prioritize stability, order, and the overarching vision in their decision-making, making choices that reinforce the structure and direction of the organization.

The interplay between leadership archetypes and leadership practice is dynamic and multifaceted, influencing leadership style, communication, and decision-making in profound ways. Leaders who engage with and understand the archetypal energies influencing their behavior can harness these forces to enhance their effectiveness, authenticity, and resonance with those they lead. This conscious engagement with archetypes empowers leaders to navigate the complexities of leadership with greater insight and wisdom, fostering environments where both individuals and organizations can thrive.

The dominant archetype of a leader plays a critical role in shaping their approach to challenges, change management, and vision setting, deeply influencing how they perceive obstacles, navigate transitions, and articulate a path forward for their organization. Each archetype brings unique strengths and perspectives to leadership, coloring the leader's responses to the dynamic landscape of modern organizational life.

Approach to Challenges

Leaders embodying the Hero archetype typically approach challenges with courage and determination, viewing them as opportunities for achievement and growth. Their proactive stance and willingness to face difficulties head-on can inspire resilience and a can-do attitude within their teams. However, this archetype's focus on conquest and victory may sometimes overlook the subtler aspects of a situation, potentially leading to overly aggressive strategies.

Conversely, leaders resonating with the Wise Old Man/Woman archetype approach challenges with reflection and insight, drawing on deep wells of knowledge and experience. They seek to understand the underlying dynamics of challenges, offering guidance and wisdom to navigate through them. This contemplative approach fosters a learning-oriented environment but may sometimes result in slower decision-making processes.

Leaders aligned with the Ruler archetype approach challenges with a focus on maintaining order and control. They prioritize the stability and sustainability of the organization, employing structured approaches to problem-solving. While this can ensure consistency and reliability, it may sometimes limit flexibility and innovation in the face of rapidly changing scenarios.

Change Management

In managing change, Hero-archetype leaders are often at the forefront, driving transformations with enthusiasm and energy. They excel at rallying their followers behind a new vision, but their focus on action may overlook the emotional and psychological impacts of change on their teams.

Wise Old Man/Woman-archetype leaders manage change by fostering understanding and consensus. They emphasize the importance of adaptation as a process of collective growth, ensuring that changes are grounded in shared values and insights. This approach builds a strong foundation for sustainable change but requires time to cultivate buy-in and alignment.

Ruler-archetype leaders manage change by carefully planning and implementing structured processes. They ensure that changes align with the organization's long-term goals and governance structures, providing clear direction and expectations. While this approach minimizes uncertainty, it may not fully engage the creative and adaptive capacities of the organization.

Vision Setting

The dominant archetype significantly influences a leader's vision setting. Hero-archetype leaders often set bold, ambitious visions that challenge the status quo and push boundaries. Their visionary narratives are marked by themes of adventure, conquest, and triumph, motivating their teams to achieve exceptional goals.

Wise Old Man/Woman-archetype leaders set visions that are reflective and inclusive, rooted in deep wisdom and a broad perspective. Their visions emphasize collective well-being, growth, and the pursuit of knowledge, inspiring their organizations towards meaningful and purposeful goals.

Ruler-archetype leaders set visions that emphasize order, stability, and prosperity. Their visions are often strategic, outlining a clear path for growth and development within a structured and controlled framework. This approach ensures alignment and coherence but may need to be more dynamic and responsive to emerging opportunities and challenges.

A leader's dominant archetype profoundly impacts their leadership style, influencing how they confront challenges, manage change, and articulate visions for the future. By understanding and consciously leveraging their archetypal strengths, leaders can navigate the complexities of leadership with greater effectiveness and authenticity, fostering organizational cultures that are resilient, adaptive, and aligned with their deepest values and aspirations.

**Application of Jungian Archetypes to Leadership Personas**

The application of Jungian archetypes to leadership personas offers leaders a profound tool for self-awareness and team dynamics management. By identifying their own archetypal patterns and recognizing the archetypes active within their teams and organizations, leaders can enhance their effectiveness, foster deeper connections, and navigate the complexities of organizational life with greater insight.

Leaders begin this journey by reflecting on their personal values, beliefs, motivations, and the narratives that have shaped their lives. This introspection can reveal the archetypal patterns that resonate most strongly with their leadership style. For instance, a leader might recognize a strong affinity with the Hero archetype if they are naturally drawn to overcoming challenges and pioneering new paths. Alternatively, a leader might identify with the Sage if they prioritize knowledge, wisdom, and guiding others.

Psychological assessments, reflective journaling, and feedback from peers and mentors can also provide valuable insights into a leader's dominant archetypes. Understanding one's archetypal patterns allows leaders to leverage their inherent strengths more consciously and address potential blind spots. For example, a Ruler archetype leader might need to cultivate flexibility and empathy to balance their natural inclination towards order and control.

Leaders can also apply Jungian archetypes to understand the dynamics within their teams and organizations better. Observing team interactions, decision-making processes, and the stories and symbols that resonate within the organizational culture can reveal the collective archetypes at play. A team that rallies around innovation and risk-taking may be influenced by the Explorer archetype, while an organization that values tradition and hierarchy may resonate with the Ruler archetype.

Identifying these collective archetypal patterns can help leaders tailor their approach to leadership, communication, and change management in ways that align with the team or organizational psyche. For instance, in an organization with a strong Caregiver archetype, emphasizing support, nurturance, and community in leadership messages can foster a sense of belonging and loyalty.

Effective leadership requires the integration and balance of different archetypal energies. Leaders should strive to develop a versatile leadership persona that can adapt to the needs of their followers and the demands of different situations. This might mean invoking the Warrior archetype in times of crisis to exhibit strength and decisiveness, while embodying the Lover archetype in moments that require empathy and connection. Leaders can promote a balanced archetypal culture within their teams and organizations by encouraging diversity in leadership styles and valuing the unique contributions of each archetype. This approach fosters a rich, dynamic organizational culture capable of navigating change and achieving its goals.

The application of Jungian archetypes to leadership personas offers a powerful framework for self-discovery and organizational insight. By identifying and embracing their archetypal patterns, leaders can enhance their authenticity, engage more deeply with their teams, and navigate the complexities of leadership with wisdom and agility. This archetypal awareness empowers leaders to create environments where diverse talents are recognized, valued, and integrated into a cohesive, purpose-driven whole.

Integrating and balancing different Jungian archetypes in their leadership approach offers leaders a nuanced strategy to enhance their effectiveness and adaptability. This process involves a conscious effort to recognize and cultivate the diverse archetypal energies within themselves and to apply these insights in leading their teams and organizations.

Leaders can start by developing a deep self-awareness of their dominant archetypal influences and understanding how these patterns manifest in their leadership style. Reflective practices such as journaling, meditation, or working with a coach can reveal which archetypes are most active and how they influence decision-making, problem-solving, and interpersonal dynamics. Recognizing one's primary archetypal influences is the first step towards cultivating a more balanced and versatile leadership approach.

Next, leaders should explore the archetypal energies that are less dominant in their personality. For instance, a leader who strongly identifies with the Ruler archetype might benefit from integrating aspects of the Creator archetype to foster innovation and flexibility. This exploration can involve seeking out new experiences, learning opportunities, or feedback that challenge the leader to grow beyond their comfort zone and develop new facets of their leadership persona.

Leaders can also apply their understanding of archetypes to recognize and value the diverse archetypal influences within their teams. By identifying which archetypes are represented among team members, leaders can tailor their communication and motivation strategies to resonate with those diverse energies. This might involve aligning tasks and roles with individuals' archetypal strengths or harnessing the collective power of multiple archetypes to tackle complex challenges.

Adapting leadership style according to the situational context is another key strategy. Different challenges and stages of organizational development may call for different archetypal energies. A leader might invoke the Warrior archetype during times of significant challenge or competition, switch to the Sage archetype when guidance and wisdom are needed or embody the Caregiver archetype to support team cohesion and morale during periods of change or uncertainty.

Fostering an organizational culture that values and integrates diverse archetypal expressions can enhance collective adaptability and effectiveness. Leaders can encourage an environment where various leadership styles, informed by different archetypes, are recognized and valued. This cultural richness ensures that the organization can respond dynamically to changing environments, leveraging the full spectrum of human capacities and perspectives.

Consciously integrating and balancing different archetypes in leadership is not a static goal but an ongoing journey of personal and professional development. It requires leaders to remain open, reflective, and committed to growth, both for themselves and their organizations. By embracing the complexity and richness of archetypal patterns, leaders can forge a path that is both deeply authentic and highly adaptable, capable of meeting the demands of an ever-evolving world with insight, creativity, and resilience.

The conscious use of archetypes in leadership can serve as a powerful tool for forging deeper connections with followers and promoting a shared sense of identity and purpose within organizations. By tapping into the universal themes and symbols that archetypes represent, leaders can communicate and lead in ways that resonate on a profound level with their teams, transcending mere transactional interactions to engage with the deeper aspirations and motivations of their followers.

Creating Resonance Through Archetypal Narratives

Leaders who skillfully weave archetypal narratives into their communication can create a strong resonance with their followers. For example, invoking the Hero's journey in the narrative of an organizational change initiative can transform the perception of the change from a source of disruption to an epic quest, imbuing it with meaning and purpose. This not only motivates followers by framing their efforts as part of a larger story but also helps them navigate the challenges of change with a sense of direction and destiny.

Fostering a Shared Sense of Identity

Archetypes can also play a crucial role in shaping organizational culture and identity. By embodying archetypal qualities that align with the organization's values and goals—such as the Caregiver's empathy in a health services company or the Explorer's innovation in a tech startup—leaders can model behaviors and attitudes that reflect the organization's core identity. This encourages followers to see themselves as part of a collective narrative, fostering a sense of belonging and shared purpose.

Enhancing Emotional Connection

The symbolic power of archetypes can enhance the emotional connection between leaders and their followers. By engaging with archetypes such as the Sage or the Mentor, leaders can offer guidance and support that addresses not just the practical aspects of work but also the emotional and developmental needs of their followers. This approach builds trust and loyalty, as followers feel seen and valued not just for their contributions but for their personal growth and well-being.

Promoting Adaptability and Creativity

The conscious use of archetypes can also promote adaptability and creativity within organizations. By encouraging followers to explore and embody different archetypal energies—such as the Creator's innovation or the Rebel's challenge to the status quo—leaders can foster a culture where diverse perspectives and approaches are valued. This not only enhances problem-solving and innovation but also ensures that the organization can adapt to changing environments with agility and resilience.

Building a Legacy

Leaders who understand and utilize archetypes can build a lasting legacy within their organizations. By aligning their leadership with timeless archetypal themes, they can leave an imprint that transcends their tenure, shaping the organization's narrative and culture in enduring ways. This legacy continues to inspire and guide future generations within the organization, ensuring that the leader's impact is felt long after they have moved on.

The conscious use of archetypes in leadership is a profound strategy for connecting with followers on a deep psychological level, fostering a shared sense of identity and purpose, and building a culture of adaptability, creativity, and resilience. By leveraging the universal power of archetypes, leaders can transcend the ordinary bounds of leadership, creating organizations that are not only effective and innovative but also rich in meaning and connectedness.

## Influence of Archetypes on Organizational Culture and Follower Perceptions

The role of archetypes in shaping organizational culture is both profound and multifaceted, influencing the values, norms, and behaviors that define the collective identity of a group. Archetypes, as universal, instinctive patterns, resonate at a deep level within the human psyche, providing a rich source of symbolism and meaning that can be harnessed to cultivate a distinctive and cohesive organizational culture.

- Archetypes influence organizational values by embodying ideals, virtues, and aspirations that can inspire and unify members. For instance, the Warrior archetype, with its emphasis on courage and perseverance, may instill values of resilience and determination in the face of challenges. Similarly, the Caregiver archetype can promote values of empathy, support, and community, encouraging a culture where members look after one another and prioritize collective well-being. By aligning organizational values with archetypal energies, leaders can foster a strong sense of purpose and identity that resonates with the deeper motivations of their teams.

- Archetypes within an organization also shape the norms and behaviors that characterize the way members interact with each other and approach their work. An organization dominated by the Creator archetype, for example, might encourage innovation, experimentation, and risk-taking as norms, fostering an environment where creativity and originality are valued and rewarded. On the other hand, an organization resonating with the Ruler archetype might emphasize order, structure, and governance, leading to norms that prioritize consistency, reliability, and adherence to established procedures.

- Archetypes deeply influence leadership styles and the modes of communication within an organization. A leader who embodies the Sage archetype might adopt a consultative and reflective leadership style, prioritizing wisdom and insight in decision-making and communication. This can create a culture of learning and development, where knowledge sharing, and mentorship are central. Conversely, a leader resonating with the Hero archetype might favor a more dynamic and assertive style, inspiring action and fostering a narrative of collective achievement and overcoming obstacles.

- Archetypes play a crucial role in facilitating group cohesion and a shared sense of identity. By invoking archetypal stories and symbols that resonate with the collective unconscious, leaders can create a powerful sense of belonging and connection among members. This shared archetypal narrative helps to define the group's identity, distinguishing it from other organizations and fostering a strong sense of pride and loyalty. The stories an organization tells about itself, its founders, its struggles, and its achievements often draw on archetypal themes, cementing a shared history and identity that guides its future.

- Archetypes can be instrumental in driving change and transformation within organizations. The archetypal theme of the journey, with its stages of departure, initiation, and return, can frame organizational change as an epic quest, imbuing the process with meaning and direction. This can help members navigate the uncertainties of change with a sense of purpose and anticipation of growth, rather than fear or resistance. Leaders can leverage archetypal symbols and narratives to articulate a vision for change that aligns with the organization's core identity and values, facilitating a smoother transition and greater alignment with the new direction.

The role of archetypes in shaping organizational culture is both powerful and pervasive. By tapping into the universal themes and symbols that archetypes represent, leaders can cultivate organizational cultures that are deeply resonant, cohesive, and aligned with their core values and objectives. This archetypal approach to culture building not only enhances organizational effectiveness but also enriches the collective experience of its members, creating a more meaningful and fulfilling workplace.

The archetypal expressions of leaders have a profound impact on how they are perceived by their followers, significantly influencing follower motivation and loyalty. These expressions, rooted in universal patterns of human experience and behavior, resonate deeply with followers, shaping their perceptions of leadership effectiveness, trustworthiness, and charisma.

When leaders embody archetypes that align with the values and aspirations of their followers, they are often seen as more authentic and inspiring. For instance, a leader who embodies the Hero archetype, demonstrating courage, resilience, and a commitment to overcoming challenges, can inspire followers to adopt a similar mindset. This shared narrative of embarking on a quest and facing adversities head-on can foster a strong sense of camaraderie and purpose among team members, boosting their motivation and dedication to the collective mission. Conversely, leaders expressing the Sage archetype, characterized by wisdom, insight, and a focus on teaching and learning, may cultivate an environment of trust and intellectual growth. Followers are likely to perceive such leaders as mentors who value their development, leading to increased engagement, loyalty, and a willingness to explore new ideas and approaches.

The Ruler archetype, with its emphasis on stability, order, and governance, can also shape follower perceptions and behaviors. Leaders who exhibit Ruler qualities are often viewed as strong and authoritative figures capable of guiding the organization towards success and prosperity. This can instill a sense of security and confidence among followers, fostering loyalty and a commitment to the vision and goals set forth by the leader. However, the impact of a leader's archetypal expression on followers is not solely determined by the archetype itself but by how well it aligns with the followers' needs, values, and the organizational context. A mismatch between the leader's archetypal expression and the followers' expectations or the organization's culture can lead to disengagement and a lack of trust. For example, a leader embodying the Warrior archetype in an organization that values collaboration and empathy above all might find it challenging to connect with their team, potentially leading to resistance or conflict.

The dynamic interplay between different archetypal expressions within a leadership team can enrich the organizational culture, offering a multifaceted approach to leadership that addresses a broader range of follower needs and aspirations. This diversity in archetypal expression can enhance the organization's adaptability, creativity, and resilience, as different situations may call for different archetypal qualities to come to the forefront.

Leaders' archetypal expressions play a critical role in shaping follower perceptions, influencing their motivation, engagement, and loyalty. By consciously aligning their archetypal expression with the needs and values of their followers and the organizational context, leaders can foster a strong, cohesive culture that empowers individuals and propels the organization towards its goals. This alignment not only enhances the effectiveness of the leader but also enriches the collective journey of growth and achievement for all members of the organization.

The potential for archetype mismatches between leaders and their organizations or teams represents a significant challenge that can impact leadership effectiveness, follower engagement, and overall organizational cohesion. Such mismatches occur when the dominant archetypal patterns expressed by a leader do not align with the prevailing archetypes, values, or expectations within the team or organizational culture. This misalignment can lead to misunderstandings, reduced morale, and resistance to leadership initiatives, undermining the leader's ability to inspire and mobilize their followers effectively.

Identifying Archetype Mismatches

The first step in addressing archetype mismatches is to recognize their existence. Leaders can do this by observing patterns of communication, feedback, and resistance within their teams. For example, a leader embodying the Warrior archetype in a context that values the Caregiver archetype might notice a disconnect in how their assertiveness is perceived, possibly being seen as aggressive rather than protective. Paying attention to the stories, symbols, and narratives that resonate within the organization can also provide insights into the dominant archetypes and whether there is a misalignment with the leader's natural archetypal expression.

Strategies for Alignment

Once a mismatch has been identified, several strategies can be employed to foster alignment between the leader's archetypal expression and the organizational culture:

1. Flexing Archetypal Expressions: Leaders can consciously adapt their archetypal expression to better fit the organizational context. This doesn't mean abandoning one's authentic leadership style but rather expanding it to include aspects of other archetypes that resonate more closely with the team or organization. For instance, a leader with a strong Ruler archetype might incorporate elements of the Sage archetype to emphasize learning and development in an organization that values continuous improvement.

2. Building Archetypal Diversity within Leadership Teams: Creating leadership teams with a diverse range of archetypal expressions can help bridge gaps between the leader's natural archetype and the organization's culture. This diversity ensures that various follower needs, and organizational values are represented and can be addressed effectively, fostering a more inclusive and adaptive leadership approach.

3. Engaging in Dialogue and Feedback: Openly discussing the role of archetypes and leadership expectations with team members can provide valuable insights into perceived mismatches and areas for alignment. This dialogue can facilitate mutual understanding and identify ways the leader and team can adapt to each other's needs and expectations, enhancing cohesion and trust.

4. Cultivating Self-Awareness and Development: Leaders can engage in continuous self-reflection and development to enhance their understanding of their own archetypal patterns and how these influence their leadership. Workshops, coaching, and reflective practices can aid leaders in exploring different facets of their personality and developing a more versatile leadership style that can adapt to varying organizational cultures and team dynamics.

5. Aligning Organizational Culture with Leadership: In some cases, it may be appropriate to gradually shift the organizational culture to better align with the leader's archetypal strengths, particularly if this alignment supports the organization's strategic direction and goals. This process involves clear communication of the vision, consistent modeling of desired behaviors, and fostering an environment that supports the cultural transformation.

Addressing archetype mismatches requires a thoughtful and multifaceted approach, emphasizing flexibility, open communication, and continuous growth. By actively seeking alignment between their archetypal expressions and the organizational culture, leaders can enhance their effectiveness, foster stronger connections with their followers, and contribute to the creation of a cohesive and resilient organizational identity.

**Case Studies**

Case Study 1: The Visionary Leader (The Magician Archetype)

A tech startup founder who has revolutionized the way we interact with digital media, embodying the Magician archetype. This leader is known for their ability to envision a future where technology enhances human connection in ways previously unimaginable.

By embodying the Magician archetype, the leader fosters an organizational culture that values innovation, transformation, and the belief that anything is possible with the right combination of technology and creativity. The leader's visionary approach inspires the team to push the boundaries of innovation, leading to the development of groundbreaking products that redefine market standards.

The culture within this organization is one of relentless pursuit of innovation, where team members are encouraged to explore unconventional ideas and take calculated risks. The leader's Magician qualities create an environment where magical transformations are part of the daily work, leading to high levels of creativity, engagement, and loyalty among employees.

Case Study 2: The Servant Leader (The Caregiver Archetype)

The CEO of a non-profit organization dedicated to solving global water scarcity, who embodies the Caregiver archetype. This leader prioritizes the well-being of communities affected by water issues and fosters a culture of service and empathy within the organization.

Through the Caregiver archetype, the leader instills a sense of purpose and compassion in the team, emphasizing the importance of service above self. This approach galvanizes the organization around a shared mission, driving efforts to innovate and collaborate on solutions that make a tangible difference in people's lives.

The organizational culture is characterized by empathy, teamwork, and a commitment to making a positive impact. The leader's embodiment of the Caregiver archetype nurtures a supportive and collaborative environment, where employees are deeply committed to the organization's mission and to each other.

Case Study 3: The Transformative Leader (The Hero Archetype)

A corporate executive who led a struggling retail company through a successful turnaround, embodying the Hero archetype. Facing intense competition and internal challenges, the leader took bold actions to reinvent the company's business model and brand.

By embracing the Hero archetype, the leader demonstrates courage, resilience, and a willingness to confront difficult truths. Their leadership transforms the company, rallying employees around a new vision and strategy that revitalizes the brand and restores profitability.

The culture within the company becomes one of resilience, innovation, and shared victory. Employees are inspired by the leader's Heroic journey, which instills a sense of pride and collective achievement. The leader's actions encourage a culture where challenges are viewed as opportunities for growth and transformation.

These case studies, while hypothetical, are inspired by the qualities and impacts associated with specific Jungian archetypes. They illustrate how leaders, by embodying these archetypes, can profoundly influence their leadership effectiveness and the culture of their organizations, driving success and transformation in diverse contexts.

We now present a case example that illustrates the power of a leader's ability to balance and transition between different archetypes in response to the evolving needs of an organization, particularly during times of change or crisis. It highlights how a nuanced understanding and application of archetypal energies can facilitate effective leadership and drive organizational transformation.

Multiple Archetype Case Example: Transformation of a Technology Company

Consider a technology company facing a significant crisis due to rapidly changing market dynamics and internal innovation challenges. The CEO, Alex, recognized the need for a comprehensive organizational transformation to stay competitive. Alex's leadership style uniquely balanced the Sage, Warrior, and

Creator archetypes, allowing for a multifaceted approach to navigating the crisis.

Phase 1: Crisis Recognition and Strategy Formulation (The Sage)
Sage Archetype Activation:

Alex began by deeply analyzing the market and internal challenges, leveraging the Sage archetype's wisdom and insight. This involved gathering extensive data, seeking expert opinions, and reflecting on the company's core competencies and mission. Alex communicated the findings and the need for change in a manner that emphasized understanding and learning, characteristic of the Sage. This approach fostered trust and openness among employees, preparing the ground for the transformation.

Phase 2: Mobilizing the Organization (The Warrior)
Warrior Archetype Activation:

With a clear strategy in place, Alex shifted to embody the Warrior archetype, making bold decisions to restructure the organization, cut underperforming projects, and invest in new technologies. Facing resistance and skepticism, Alex demonstrated resilience, a hallmark of the Warrior, championing the change despite the obstacles, and instilling a sense of urgency and commitment across the company.

Phase 3: Fostering Innovation and Renewal (The Creator)
Creator Archetype Activation:

Moving beyond the immediate crisis, Alex then embraced the Creator archetype, focusing on fostering a culture of innovation and creativity. This involved launching new initiatives to explore emerging technologies and encouraging cross-functional teams to develop innovative solutions. Alex empowered employees to take ownership of the transformation process, encouraging risk-taking and experimentation, essential qualities of the Creator archetype. This empowerment led to the development of breakthrough products and services that revitalized the company's market position.

Analysis and Impact

By effectively balancing the Sage, Warrior, and Creator archetypes, Alex navigated the company through a critical period of transformation. The Sage archetype's focus on wisdom and insight ensured that the change was grounded in a deep understanding of the company's challenges and opportunities. The Warrior archetype's emphasis on courage and action provided the necessary drive and determination to implement difficult decisions swiftly. Finally, the Creator archetype's orientation towards innovation and creativity fostered a culture of renewal, enabling the company to emerge from the crisis stronger and more competitive.

Organizational Impact

- The balanced application of these archetypes led to a renewed organizational culture that valued learning, resilience, and innovation.

- Employee engagement and loyalty increased as staff felt part of a meaningful journey of transformation and were empowered to contribute creatively to the company's renewal.

- The company successfully navigated the crisis, emerging as a leader in innovation within its industry, with improved financial performance and market share.

We conclude this section with one more case example of initial misalignment of a leader's archetypal persona with the organizational needs.

Misalignment Case Example: The Dissonant Turnaround Specialist

Jordan, a seasoned executive known for their turnaround expertise, was brought in to lead a struggling consumer goods company back to profitability. Jordan's leadership style was heavily influenced by the Warrior archetype, characterized by bold decisions, a focus on discipline, and an aggressive approach to change. While effective in crisis situations, this archetypal persona was at odds with the company's deeply ingrained Caregiver culture, which valued employee well-being, long-term relationships with partners, and a nurturing approach to management.

Challenges Arising from Misalignment

Jordan's Warrior-driven initiatives for rapid restructuring and cost-cutting were met with significant resistance from employees who felt these actions contradicted the company's values of care and loyalty. Morale plummeted as the workforce struggled to reconcile the new leadership style with the established organizational culture. The perceived disregard for the company's caregiving ethos eroded trust between Jordan and the team. Key talent began to leave, fearing that the organizational changes would strip away the supportive environment they valued. The aggressive internal changes also started to affect the company's brand, which was built on community and customer care. Stakeholders expressed concerns that the company was moving away from its core identity.

Addressing the Misalignment

The turning point came when Jordan recognized the misalignment between their Warrior approach and the company's Caregiver culture. This realization was prompted by feedback from a company-wide engagement survey and interventions by HR and a trusted advisor. Jordan embarked on a journey to integrate more of the Caregiver archetype into their leadership style, while still maintaining the decisive qualities of the Warrior where necessary. Jordan initiated a series of open forums and town hall meetings to better understand employee concerns and to communicate the rationale behind the restructuring efforts, emphasizing the ultimate goal of preserving the company and its values. Jordan began to balance the Warrior's assertiveness with the Caregiver's empathy, involving employees in decision-making processes and making more transparent efforts to mitigate the impacts of change on the workforce. Initiatives were introduced to reinforce the company's caregiving values, including enhanced support programs for employees affected by the restructuring and a renewed focus on community engagement and customer care.

Outcome and Lessons Learned

The conscious effort to balance the Warrior and Caregiver archetypes led to a gradual restoration of trust and morale within the company. Employees began to see the changes not as a departure from the company's core values but as necessary steps to preserve its mission and identity in the long term. The brand's integrity was maintained, and the company eventually returned to profitability, with a more resilient and adaptive culture.

Key Insights

This case highlights the importance of aligning leadership style with organizational culture and values. A misalignment, especially during times of change, can exacerbate challenges rather than mitigate them. It underscores the necessity for leaders to possess a degree of archetypal fluidity, enabling them to adapt their approach to meet the needs of their organization and its people. The case also illustrates the power of feedback and self-reflection in identifying misalignments and the potential for transformative growth when leaders are willing to integrate diverse aspects of their persona to navigate complex organizational landscapes effectively.

**Leveraging Archetypes for Effective Leadership**

Leveraging archetypes for effective leadership requires a nuanced understanding of the symbolic and unconscious influences that underpin leadership dynamics. To harness the power of archetypes in leadership practice, leaders must embark on a journey of self-awareness, beginning with introspection to uncover their dominant archetypal influences. This self-exploration, aided by tools such as personality assessments and feedback from colleagues, reveals the archetypal patterns shaping their leadership style.

Leaders should also immerse themselves in the study of archetypal symbols and themes, gaining familiarity with archetypes like the Hero, Sage, Warrior, and Caregiver. This knowledge enables them to recognize which archetypes resonate with their personal leadership journey and identify those that are active within their team or organization.

Observing archetypal dynamics within the team is crucial. Leaders must pay attention to the stories, myths, and symbols that hold significance within their organization, noting how team members embody different archetypes. This awareness allows leaders to tailor their approach to complement and enhance these dynamics, fostering a cohesive and motivated team. Communicating with archetypal resonance involves using stories and metaphors that tap into universal themes when articulating vision, values, and goals. Such communication deepens the emotional and psychological connection with the team, making leadership messages more impactful.

Balancing archetypal energies is essential, as no single archetype captures the full spectrum of effective leadership. Leaders must be adaptable, embodying different archetypes as situations demand. This flexibility enables them to respond appropriately to various challenges and opportunities. Promoting archetypal diversity within the team enriches problem-solving, innovation, and adaptability. Leaders should encourage team members to explore and express their unique archetypal influences, leveraging these for personal and professional growth.

Integrating shadow aspects, the traits or impulses typically suppressed, leads to more authentic and holistic leadership. Acknowledging these aspects prevents unconscious biases or behaviors from undermining leadership effectiveness. Leaders must also focus on promoting personal and collective growth, encouraging team members to explore their archetypal influences and how these can contribute to their development. This emphasis on growth fosters an environment where personal development and professional excellence are intertwined.

Continuous reflection on the effectiveness of an archetypal leadership approach is vital. Leaders should remain open to feedback and willing to adjust their strategies to better align with the needs of their organization and its members. By thoughtfully engaging with archetypes, leaders can deepen their effectiveness, forge stronger connections with their teams, and cultivate a culture rich in meaning, motivation, and shared purpose. This approach offers a profound way to navigate the complexities of organizational life, unlocking transformative growth and success.

Developing a nuanced and archetypally informed leadership style that resonates with diverse followers and adapts to changing circumstances requires a multifaceted approach, blending introspection, adaptability, and strategic communication. Leaders must embark on a journey of self-discovery to understand the archetypal influences that shape their leadership. This involves deep reflection on personal motivations, strengths, and weaknesses, perhaps facilitated by psychological assessments, reflective practices, or coaching. Such self-awareness enables leaders to recognize the archetypes they naturally embody and how these influence their interactions with others.

Simultaneously, leaders should strive to understand the archetypal dynamics within their teams and organizations. This can be achieved by observing the narratives, symbols, and behaviors that are prevalent and noting how these elements influence team cohesion, motivation, and organizational culture. Such awareness allows leaders to identify the archetypal needs of their followers and the broader organizational context, informing their approach to leadership.

To resonate with diverse followers, leaders must cultivate the ability to flexibly embody different archetypes as situations demand. This doesn't mean being inauthentic but rather expanding one's leadership repertoire to include qualities from various archetypes that may not be as naturally predominant. For instance, a leader who primarily identifies with the Warrior archetype might learn to incorporate aspects of the Caregiver or Sage when those qualities are needed to support team development or navigate complex challenges.

Effective communication is crucial in an archetypally informed leadership style. Leaders should harness the power of archetypal stories and symbols to craft messages that speak to the collective unconscious of their followers, thereby forging a deeper emotional and psychological connection. This might involve framing organizational goals in terms of a hero's journey, emphasizing the collective quest and the challenges to be overcome, or invoking the imagery of a community or family to strengthen bonds and foster a sense of belonging.

Embracing the shadow aspects of one's dominant archetypes is also vital. By acknowledging and integrating these often overlooked or suppressed parts of the self, leaders can prevent unconscious biases or negative behaviors from undermining their effectiveness. This process enhances authenticity and allows for a more holistic expression of leadership.

Promoting a culture of archetypal diversity and inclusion within the organization further enriches the leadership approach. By valuing and encouraging the expression of a wide range of archetypal qualities among team members, leaders can create a dynamic and adaptable organizational culture that leverages the full spectrum of human potential.

Continuous learning and development are key to maintaining a nuanced and archetypally informed leadership style. Leaders should remain open to new insights about themselves and the archetypal dimensions of leadership, seeking out opportunities for growth through education, reflection, and dialogue with others.

Developing an archetypally informed leadership style that resonates with diverse followers and adapts to changing circumstances involves a deep engagement with both the inner world of the leader and the outer world of the team and organization. By cultivating self-awareness, flexibility, strategic communication, and a culture of inclusion, leaders can navigate the complexities of modern leadership with wisdom, empathy, and effectiveness.

Using archetypal awareness to enhance personal growth and leadership development involves a journey into the deeper aspects of the self and the collective unconscious, offering a rich pathway for understanding and transformation. This process starts with cultivating a deep sense of self-awareness, recognizing the archetypal patterns that influence one's thoughts, feelings, and behaviors. Engaging in reflective practices such as meditation, journaling, or psychotherapy can provide insights into these unconscious influences, revealing the archetypes that play a significant role in one's life and leadership style.

To further develop archetypal awareness, studying the myths, stories, and symbols associated with various archetypes can be incredibly enlightening. These narratives offer a mirror to reflect on personal experiences and challenges, providing a symbolic language for understanding complex emotions and situations. By exploring these stories, leaders can identify with certain archetypes more strongly than others, gaining clarity on their innate tendencies, strengths, and areas for growth.

Integrating shadow aspects is another crucial recommendation for using archetypal awareness in personal growth. Every archetype has its shadow side, representing the qualities and behaviors that are often denied or suppressed. Acknowledging and embracing these shadow aspects can lead to a more balanced and authentic expression of the self, reducing internal conflicts and enhancing interpersonal relationships.

Applying archetypal insights in everyday leadership practice involves consciously embodying the positive qualities of various archetypes in response to different situations. For example, adopting the qualities of the Caregiver can enhance empathy and supportiveness, while the Warrior archetype can inspire courage and decisiveness. This flexible approach allows leaders to respond more effectively to the needs of their teams and the demands of the environment.

Creating a dialogue around archetypes within teams and organizations can also foster a deeper collective understanding and connection. Leaders can facilitate discussions about the archetypal themes and dynamics at play within the group, encouraging team members to explore their own archetypal influences. This shared exploration can strengthen team cohesion, enhance mutual understanding, and promote a more inclusive and dynamic organizational culture.

Ongoing learning and reflection are essential for sustaining personal growth and leadership development through archetypal awareness. Leaders should remain open to new insights and perspectives, continually revisiting their understanding of archetypes and their application in both personal and professional contexts. Engaging with a community of like-minded individuals, attending workshops, or seeking mentorship can provide valuable support and inspiration on this journey.

Leveraging archetypal awareness for personal growth and leadership development offers a profound and transformative approach to understanding the self and leading others. By cultivating self-awareness, integrating shadow aspects, applying archetypal insights in practice, fostering collective exploration, and committing to ongoing learning, leaders can navigate the complexities of leadership with greater wisdom, authenticity, and effectiveness.

## Conclusion

Carl Jung's theories on archetypes offer profound insights into the psychological underpinnings of leadership and organizational dynamics. At the heart of Jung's work is the concept of the collective unconscious, a shared psychic reservoir that holds the experiences and patterns common to all humanity. This collective unconscious is home to archetypes, universal symbols, and themes that shape human behavior and perceptions.

One of the key insights from Jung's theories is the understanding that leadership and organizational cultures are deeply influenced by these archetypal patterns. Leaders often embody specific archetypes—such as the Hero, the Sage, or the Ruler—that resonate with their followers and shape their leadership style. These archetypal influences can impact a leader's approach to decision-making, problem-solving, and how they inspire and mobilize their teams. Archetypes also play a critical role in shaping organizational culture. The dominant archetypes within an organization influence its values, norms, and behaviors, creating a shared sense of identity and purpose. For example, an organization with a strong Caregiver archetype may prioritize employee well-being and community involvement, while one influenced by the Creator archetype might focus on innovation and creativity.

Jung's theories highlight the importance of understanding and balancing these archetypal energies. Leaders who can recognize and integrate various archetypal qualities can respond more effectively to different situations and challenges, fostering a more adaptable and resilient leadership style. This archetypal awareness can also help leaders navigate the complex dynamics of organizational change, ensuring that transformations align with the deep-seated values and motivations of their teams. His concept of the shadow—the aspects of the self that are often suppressed or ignored—offers valuable lessons for leadership development. By acknowledging and integrating their shadow aspects, leaders can achieve greater authenticity and wholeness, reducing the risk of unconscious biases or behaviors that could undermine their effectiveness.

In applying Jung's insights to leadership and organizational dynamics, it becomes clear that fostering an environment that recognizes and values the diversity of archetypal expressions can enhance organizational health and performance. Encouraging team members to explore and express their unique archetypal influences can lead to a richer, more dynamic organizational culture, characterized by creativity, adaptability, and a deep sense of connectedness.

Jung's theories on archetypes provide a powerful framework for understanding the psychological dimensions of leadership and organizational life. By embracing the complexity and richness of archetypal patterns, leaders can cultivate more authentic, effective, and resilient forms of leadership that resonate with the fundamental human experiences and aspirations of their followers.

Engaging with archetypes holds transformative potential for leaders seeking to deepen their impact and foster more cohesive and inspired organizations. This engagement offers a journey into the collective unconscious, where the universal patterns of human experience reside. By tapping into these archetypal energies, leaders can unlock deeper layers of meaning and motivation, both within themselves and among their followers, leading to profound changes in leadership style, organizational culture, and collective achievement.

The transformative journey begins with leaders developing a deeper self-awareness of their own archetypal influences. This introspection allows them to understand the foundational aspects of their leadership identity, including their strengths, weaknesses, and the instinctual strategies they employ in navigating challenges. Such awareness not only enhances personal growth but also enables leaders to more authentically connect with their followers, as they embody archetypal qualities that resonate on a universal level.

Engaging with archetypes enables leaders to communicate more effectively. Archetypal themes and narratives speak to the deep-seated experiences and aspirations common to all humanity, transcending cultural and linguistic barriers. By framing their vision, values, and goals in terms of these universal stories, leaders can inspire and mobilize their organizations with messages that strike a chord across diverse groups, fostering a shared sense of purpose and identity.

The transformative power of archetypes also extends to organizational dynamics and culture. Leaders who understand the archetypal patterns at play within their teams and the broader organization can skillfully navigate and influence these dynamics. They can cultivate an environment that honors diverse archetypal expressions, leading to a more inclusive and dynamic culture. This recognition of the full spectrum of human potential encourages innovation, resilience, and a strong sense of community, as team members feel valued and understood at a fundamental level.

Working with archetypes equips leaders to manage change and transformation more effectively. By identifying the archetypal energies that need to be activated to support growth and renewal, leaders can guide their organizations through transitions in ways that align with deep psychological needs and aspirations. This approach not only facilitates smoother change processes but also ensures that transformations are meaningful and sustainable, resonating with the core identity of the organization.

The engagement with archetypes fosters a leadership approach that is both adaptable and grounded. Leaders become capable of flexibly embodying different archetypal qualities as circumstances require, while also maintaining a connection to timeless principles and values. This balance between adaptability and authenticity is crucial in today's rapidly changing world, enabling leaders to navigate complexity with confidence and wisdom.

Exploring the archetypal dimensions of leadership and considering the unconscious influences on leadership style and organizational culture can open up new avenues for growth, understanding, and effectiveness. This exploration invites leaders into a deeper engagement with the symbolic and mythic underpinnings of human behavior and organizational life, enriching their approach to leadership and fostering a more dynamic and cohesive organizational culture.

Understanding your leadership through the lens of archetypes allows you to connect with the foundational elements of human motivation and psyche. It offers a framework to comprehend the deeper motivations of your actions and decisions, as well as those of your team members. By identifying with archetypes such as the Sage, Warrior, or Caregiver, you can gain insights into your natural strengths and areas where you may need to develop further.

Reflecting on the unconscious influences on your leadership involves acknowledging that much of what drives behavior and decision-making lies below the surface of conscious awareness. Engaging with these unconscious aspects can reveal hidden sources of conflict, resilience, and inspiration, both within yourself and your organization. This awareness can lead to more authentic and effective leadership, as it encompasses a broader understanding of human complexity. Considering the impact of archetypal patterns on organizational culture encourages a holistic view of how shared values, beliefs, and behaviors are formed. It highlights the role of symbolic narratives and myths in shaping the collective identity of an organization, offering pathways to cultivate a culture that resonates deeply with its members and aligns with the organization's mission and vision.

Leaders are encouraged to embark on this journey of archetypal exploration with curiosity and openness. It is a process that invites continuous learning and reflection, requiring a willingness to look beyond the obvious and to engage with the rich tapestry of human experience that influences leadership and organizational dynamics.

Resources such as books, workshops, and coaching can provide guidance and support in navigating the archetypal landscape. Engaging in dialogues with mentors, peers, and team members about the role of archetypes in leadership and organizational life can also enrich this exploration, offering diverse perspectives and deepening collective understanding.

Exploring the archetypal dimensions of your leadership and the unconscious influences on your leadership style and organizational culture is not just an academic exercise. It is a transformative journey that can enhance your effectiveness as a leader, deepen your connections with others, and foster an organizational culture that is vibrant, resilient, and aligned with the deepest aspirations of its members. This journey into the archetypal and unconscious realms of leadership holds the potential for profound personal and organizational transformation.

# Chapter 2: Alfred Adler and Power Dynamics

Alfred Adler, an Austrian medical doctor and psychotherapist, is renowned for his significant contributions to psychology through the founding of Individual Psychology, marking a pivotal departure from the Freudian psychoanalytic tradition. Born in 1870, Adler's early experiences, including his own health challenges and a keen observation of social dynamics, profoundly influenced his psychological theories. Diverging from Freud's emphasis on the sexual bases of psychological disorders, Adler introduced a holistic approach that considers the individual within the broader context of society and relationships.

Central to Adler's theoretical framework is the concept of social interest, an innate potential for cooperation and contribution to the welfare of others. He posited that developing this social interest is crucial for personal and communal well-being, suggesting that a lack of social interest is at the root of many psychological and social problems. Adler introduced the idea that feelings of inferiority, experienced universally, serve as a primary motivator for individuals. These feelings, stemming from real or perceived shortcomings, propel individuals to strive for superiority or success as a means of compensation and self-assertion.

Adler emphasized that this drive for superiority should not be understood in terms of personal aggrandizement at the expense of others. Instead, he envisioned it as a healthy aspiration toward self-improvement and societal contribution, moderated by social interest. According to Adler, when this drive is coupled with a genuine concern for the welfare of others, it leads to constructive and fulfilling life pursuits.

Adler's insights into power dynamics, especially his exploration of how feelings of inferiority influence personal and professional relationships, offer valuable perspectives for understanding leadership and organizational behavior. His theories shed light on the psychological underpinnings of power struggles, the importance of fostering a sense of belonging and significance among team members, and the role of leadership in nurturing an environment where individuals feel valued and empowered to contribute to collective goals.

In the context of leadership and organizational dynamics, Adler's emphasis on social interest and the constructive management of power dynamics encourages leaders to cultivate communities of practice that are characterized by mutual respect, cooperation, and a shared commitment to the common good. By applying Adlerian principles, leaders can address and mitigate the negative aspects of power dynamics, such as competition and dominance, and instead promote a culture of inclusivity, empowerment, and collective achievement.

This chapter will delve deeper into Adler's theories, exploring their relevance to contemporary leadership challenges and offering insights on harnessing these principles to foster healthier, more dynamic, and more cohesive organizations. Through an Adlerian lens, we will examine practical strategies for leaders to navigate power dynamics effectively, enhance their leadership impact, and contribute to the development of a positive organizational culture.

**Adler's Contributions to Understanding Power**

Alfred Adler's perspective on power significantly diverges from traditional views that equate power with domination or control over others. Instead, Adler sees power as intricately linked to the individual's striving for superiority, a concept that he posits is rooted in the universal experience of feeling inferior or inadequate in some aspect of life. This striving for superiority, according to Adler, is not about surpassing others in status or success but about overcoming one's own feelings of inferiority through personal development and contribution to the welfare of others.

In Adler's view, power dynamics within a social context are influenced by the individual's desire to achieve a sense of competence and self-worth. This desire is seen as a fundamental driving force behind human behavior, shaping our interactions with others and our approach to leadership and authority. Adler emphasizes that the healthy expression of this drive is directed towards social interest—using one's capabilities and positions of influence not for personal aggrandizement but for the betterment of the community.

His concept of compensatory behavior further illuminates his understanding of power. Individuals often engage in compensatory behaviors to overcome their real or perceived inferiorities. In a leadership context, this can manifest as a leader's desire to assert authority or control as a means to compensate for feelings of inadequacy. However, Adler warns against the overcompensation that can lead to an authoritarian leadership style, arguing instead for a balanced approach that fosters cooperation and mutual respect. He introduces the idea of the "will to power" as a potential pitfall when it becomes detached from social interest. In such cases, the striving for superiority may turn into a quest for power over others, leading to destructive power dynamics within organizations. This underscores the importance of developing a strong sense of social interest and community feeling among leaders and team members alike, as a counterbalance to the potentially divisive aspects of power.

The Adlerian perspective suggests that effective leadership and healthy organizational cultures are characterized by an emphasis on collaboration, empathy, and a shared sense of purpose. Leaders who understand and apply Adler's insights into power dynamics can cultivate an environment where power is viewed not as a means of individual dominance but as a collective resource for achieving common goals. Such leaders use their influence to empower others, encouraging personal and professional growth and fostering a sense of belonging and significance within the team.

His contributions to understanding power challenge conventional notions and offer a nuanced framework for navigating power dynamics in a social context. By recognizing the interplay between feelings of inferiority, the striving for superiority, and the role of social interest, leaders can better understand their own motivations and the dynamics within their organizations. This understanding enables leaders to harness power constructively, promoting a culture of mutual respect, collaboration, and shared success.

Alfred Adler's views on power dynamics present a nuanced framework that can profoundly influence leadership practice, particularly in how power is utilized to achieve personal and collective goals. His theory, which positions the striving for superiority and social interest at the heart of human motivation, offers leaders a roadmap for harnessing power in ways that foster individual fulfillment and collective success.

Personal Goals and the Striving for Superiority

In Adler's framework, the striving for superiority is seen as a natural part of the human condition, driven by an innate desire to overcome feelings of inferiority. For leaders, this striving can be a powerful motivator toward personal development and excellence. However, Adler cautions against interpreting superiority as dominance over others. Instead, he advocates for a leadership approach that sees power as a tool for self-improvement and the achievement of personal goals that are aligned with the broader welfare of the community. Leaders can apply Adler's insights by setting personal goals that not only advance their careers but also contribute positively to their teams and organizations. This might involve seeking leadership roles that allow for the implementation of innovative practices that benefit employees, or pursuing personal development that enhances one's ability to mentor and support others.

Collective Goals and Social Interest

Adler's emphasis on social interest as a counterbalance to the striving for superiority is particularly relevant to leadership. He suggests that true power lies not in authority over others but in the ability to inspire, motivate, and uplift those one leads. This perspective shifts the focus from power as control to power as influence—a resource for achieving collective goals. Leaders can foster a culture of social interest within their organizations by prioritizing team success over individual achievements, encouraging collaboration, and recognizing contributions that advance the collective good. This approach not only enhances team cohesion but also elevates the organization's capacity to achieve its objectives.

Navigating Power Dynamics

Adler's views also offer guidance on navigating the inherent power dynamics within leadership roles. By understanding power as a manifestation of the striving for superiority, leaders can become more mindful of how their actions and decisions impact others. This awareness encourages a leadership style characterized by empathy, fairness, and respect—qualities that mitigate the negative aspects of power dynamics, such as competition and conflict. Adlerian leadership emphasizes the importance of developing a sense of belonging and significance among team members. Leaders can achieve this by creating opportunities for meaningful participation, valuing diverse perspectives, and fostering an environment where everyone feels empowered to contribute to the organization's success.

Empowering Others

Adler's theory highlights the transformative potential of empowering others. Leaders who use their power to support the growth and development of their team members not only enhance individual capabilities but also strengthen the organization as a whole. This empowerment can take many forms, from providing resources and opportunities for professional development to encouraging innovation and risk-taking within a supportive framework.

Adler's views on power dynamics offer valuable insights for leaders seeking to navigate the complexities of modern organizational life. By balancing the striving for superiority with a deep commitment to social interest, leaders can use their power to achieve both personal and collective goals. This Adlerian approach to leadership not only enhances individual fulfillment and team performance but also contributes to building more vibrant, resilient, and inclusive organizations.

**Striving for Superiority in Leadership**

The concept of striving for superiority, central to Alfred Adler's psychological theories, offers a nuanced understanding of the motivational forces behind leadership ambition. Adler posited that this striving is a fundamental human drive, originating from feelings of inferiority and the desire to overcome them. These feelings of inferiority, which Adler believed every individual experiences to some extent, stem from perceived shortcomings, whether physical, psychological, or social. The striving for superiority is thus an inherent attempt to transform these feelings into a force for personal development, achievement, and self-improvement.

In the context of leadership, this striving can be seen as a significant motivator behind a leader's ambition and their pursuit of success. It propels leaders to set high goals, persist in the face of challenges, and continuously seek ways to enhance their skills and capabilities. However, Adler made a crucial distinction between mere personal gain and a more holistic approach to superiority. He emphasized that the healthiest and most beneficial form of this striving is not directed towards surpassing others for self-aggrandizement but towards contributing to the community and advancing collective goals—a concept he termed "social interest."

For leaders, the relevance of striving for superiority lies in its ability to drive ambition in a way that aligns personal success with the welfare of others. Leaders motivated by a balanced form of this striving are likely to:

- Pursue Excellence: They set high standards for themselves and their organizations, driven by an internal desire to improve and make meaningful contributions.

- Foster Resilience: The understanding that challenges and setbacks are opportunities for growth fosters a resilient mindset, encouraging leaders to persist and learn from difficulties rather than be discouraged by them.

- Encourage Innovation: The drive to overcome feelings of inferiority can lead to innovative thinking, as leaders seek creative solutions and new paths to success.

- Cultivate Empathy: Recognizing their own struggles with inferiority helps leaders empathize with others, fostering a leadership style characterized by supportiveness and understanding.

- Promote Collaboration: By valuing social interest, leaders motivated by striving for superiority see the importance of teamwork and collective achievement, encouraging a culture of cooperation and mutual support.

- Inspire Others: Leaders who embody this striving in a balanced way serve as role models, inspiring their teams with their dedication to personal growth and their commitment to the greater good.

The concept of striving for superiority, when understood and applied within Adler's framework of social interest, becomes a powerful tool for leadership motivation and ambition. It encourages leaders to navigate their paths to success in ways that not only fulfill their personal aspirations but also contribute positively to their teams, organizations, and the broader community. This approach to leadership not only achieves superior results but also cultivates a legacy of positive impact and meaningful change.

The concept of striving for superiority, as introduced by Alfred Adler, holds profound implications for leadership, manifesting in ways that can be both constructive and destructive. This dynamic plays a critical role in shaping leadership styles, influencing decision-making processes, and guiding ethical considerations.

Constructive Manifestations

1. Personal and Professional Growth: Constructively, striving for superiority leads to continuous personal and professional development. Leaders who channel this drive positively are committed to learning, self-improvement, and acquiring new skills. This not only enhances their competency but also serves as a model for lifelong learning within their organizations.

2. Innovation and Creativity: A healthy manifestation of this striving encourages innovation and creativity. Leaders motivated by a desire to improve and contribute meaningfully to their field are more likely to pursue novel solutions to problems, fostering a culture of innovation that can propel the organization forward.

3. Empowerment and Development of Others: When leaders focus their striving for superiority on lifting others, it leads to empowerment and development within their teams. By investing in their team's growth and recognizing their potential, leaders can create an environment where everyone feels valued and motivated to contribute their best.

4. Ethical Leadership and Social Responsibility: Leaders who balance their ambition with social interest demonstrate ethical leadership. They make decisions that not only advance organizational goals but also consider the welfare of employees, communities, and the broader society. This approach fosters trust and respect, enhancing the leader's and the organization's reputation.

Destructive Manifestations

1.  Excessive Competition and Domination: Striving for superiority becomes destructive when it manifests as a need to dominate or outperform others at any cost. This can lead to a toxic work environment characterized by excessive competition, undermining collaboration, and eroding trust among team members.

2.  Neglect of Ethical Considerations: In its destructive form, the pursuit of superiority may lead leaders to prioritize success over ethical considerations, making decisions that benefit the organization or themselves at the expense of others' well-being or ethical standards.

3.  Resistance to Feedback and Learning: Leaders who are overly focused on asserting their superiority may become resistant to feedback, viewing it as a challenge to their authority rather than an opportunity for growth. This can stifle personal development and innovation within the organization.

4.  Burnout and Unsustainable Practices: Destructive striving can also lead to burnout, both for the leader and their team. Leaders may push themselves and their teams too hard in pursuit of success, adopting unsustainable practices that harm long-term organizational health.

Balancing Constructive and Destructive Aspects

For leaders, the key to harnessing the constructive potential of striving for superiority lies in self-awareness and the deliberate cultivation of social interest. Reflecting on one's motivations, recognizing the impact of one's leadership style on others, and prioritizing ethical decision-making are essential steps. Leaders can balance their ambition with empathy, collaboration, and a commitment to the common good.

Incorporating regular feedback mechanisms, fostering open communication, and creating a culture that values ethical behavior and mutual support can help mitigate the destructive tendencies of striving for superiority. Moreover, leaders can seek mentorship and engage in continuous learning to navigate the complexities of leadership with a balanced and ethical approach.

While striving for superiority is a natural and powerful motivator in leadership, its impact depends on how it is channeled. By recognizing and mitigating its potential destructive manifestations, leaders can leverage this drive constructively to foster personal growth, ethical leadership, and organizational success.

## The Feeling of Community and Leadership

Alfred Adler introduced the concept of Gemeinschaftsgefühl, often translated as social interest or community feeling, as a fundamental aspect of human psychology. He considered it not just a counterbalance but an essential complement to the striving for superiority. For Adler, social interest embodies the innate potential for cooperation, empathy, and a sense of belonging to a larger community. It's the drive that motivates individuals to contribute positively to society and to care for the welfare of others. This concept underscores the importance of social connectedness and mutual support, suggesting that true personal fulfillment and societal progress cannot be achieved through individual achievements alone but through contributions to the common good.

In leadership, the notion of Gemeinschaftsgefühl introduces a vital perspective on how leaders can cultivate environments that nurture collective success and well-being. Leaders who embody social interest prioritize the development and empowerment of their teams, recognizing that the organization's success is intrinsically linked to the well-being of its members. They understand that leadership is not about asserting dominance or achieving personal glory but about fostering a sense of community and shared purpose.

Implications for Leadership:

- Empathetic Leadership: Social interest encourages leaders to adopt an empathetic approach, considering the perspectives, needs, and aspirations of their team members. This fosters a supportive and inclusive organizational culture where individuals feel valued and understood.

- Collaborative Decision-Making: By prioritizing the community's welfare, leaders inspired by social interest are more likely to engage in collaborative decision-making processes. They recognize the importance of diverse viewpoints and the collective wisdom of the team in navigating challenges and identifying opportunities.

- Ethical Considerations: Gemeinschaftsgefühl reinforces the ethical dimensions of leadership. Leaders who embody social interest are committed to fairness, justice, and the ethical implications of their decisions, not just for their organization but for the wider community and environment.

- Fostering Team Cohesion: A strong sense of social interest helps to build team cohesion and a positive working environment. Leaders can create a sense of belonging and purpose that transcends individual tasks, aligning the team around shared goals and values.

- Sustainable Success: Leadership grounded in social interest is oriented towards sustainable success. It considers the long-term impacts of decisions on people and the planet, aiming for outcomes that are beneficial not only for the organization but also for society at large.

- Resilience and Adaptability: In times of change or crisis, a community feeling can be a source of resilience and adaptability. Leaders who foster a strong sense of togetherness and mutual support find their teams more capable of navigating uncertainties and emerging stronger.

Adler's concept of Gemeinschaftsgefühl or social interest offers a profound insight into the essence of effective leadership. It suggests that the most impactful leaders are those who go beyond mere personal or organizational ambitions to embrace a broader vision of contributing to the welfare of the community and society. This approach not only enriches the leader's personal growth and sense of fulfillment but also cultivates a more cohesive, ethical, and resilient organization.

A strong sense of community feeling, or Gemeinschaftsgefühl, profoundly shapes leadership practices, steering them towards prioritizing collaboration, empathy, and social responsibility. This ethos, rooted in Alfred Adler's psychological theories, transforms leadership from a mere exercise in authority to a deeply relational and socially conscious endeavor. When leaders embody this sense of connectedness to the larger community, it influences every facet of their leadership, from team engagement to decision-making and the organization's societal impact.

Leaders who view collaboration as a core value create an environment where teamwork and collective effort are celebrated. They recognize that bringing people together to share ideas and work jointly not only enhances creativity and problem-solving but also solidifies a culture where shared goals are the focal point of organizational efforts. Such an approach naturally cultivates a workspace where diversity of thought is valued, and the synergy of different talents is recognized as a key driver of success.

Empathy becomes a cornerstone of leadership for those attuned to community feeling. This empathetic stance enables leaders to connect with their team members on a personal level, acknowledging their needs, emotions, and aspirations. This not only builds trust and strengthens loyalty but also ensures that the work environment is supportive and nurturing. An empathetic leader is adept at resolving conflicts, inspiring their team, and fostering a positive organizational climate where everyone is motivated to contribute their best.

A commitment to social responsibility underscores the leadership practices of those guided by a strong sense of community feeling. Such leaders ensure that their organization's activities positively contribute to societal welfare. They are mindful of their impact on the environment and communities and actively seek ways to address broader social challenges through ethical business practices. This focus on social responsibility not only elevates the organization's societal contribution but also reinforces its reputation as a force for good. To embed these values into organizational practice, leaders can foster team building across different departments, encouraging a culture where cross-functional collaboration is the norm. They can practice active listening, creating spaces for employees to express their ideas and concerns, ensuring that everyone feels heard and valued. Promoting diversity and inclusion is another critical aspect, ensuring all team members feel welcomed and appreciated, thereby enriching the organizational culture with a variety of perspectives.

Leading by example in social responsibility, leaders can inspire their organizations to engage with social and environmental causes, demonstrating a personal commitment to making a difference. Additionally, educating and empowering employees about the impact of their work on society encourages a collective movement towards sustainable and ethical practices. Integrating a strong sense of community feeling into leadership practices does more than just enhance organizational efficiency; it fosters a leadership style that is both compassionate and socially aware. Such leaders not only drive their organizations towards success but also contribute significantly to building a more equitable, responsible, and sustainable world. This approach to leadership, therefore, is not just about achieving business objectives but about nurturing a community of individuals who are committed to contributing positively to the broader society.

**Adlerian Concepts in Leadership Contexts**

Delving deeper into Alfred Adler's theories reveals their profound implications for leadership and organizational dynamics, particularly in the nuanced management of power and fostering of a cooperative culture. Adler's insights into the human psyche provide a compelling lens through which to examine and refine leadership practices, emphasizing the balance between individual aspirations and communal well-being.

The concept of striving for superiority, when contextualized within the leadership domain, extends beyond mere personal achievement. It encapsulates a leader's drive to elevate their organization, innovate, and break new ground. Yet, Adler's perspective urges leaders to channel this drive into avenues that benefit the broader community, not just their personal or organizational success. This nuanced understanding encourages leaders to reflect on their motivations and the outcomes of their leadership, steering them towards practices that uplift others and contribute to collective advancement.

Adler's emphasis on social interest as a cornerstone of healthy human development translates into a leadership approach that values empathy, collaboration, and mutual support. This principle challenges leaders to look beyond conventional metrics of success, advocating for a leadership style that is deeply rooted in understanding, supporting, and empowering team members. It suggests that the true measure of leadership effectiveness lies in the ability to foster an environment where individuals feel connected, valued, and motivated to contribute to shared goals.

In managing power dynamics, Adlerian concepts offer a blueprint for a more democratic and inclusive form of leadership. This approach recognizes the potential within each team member, encouraging leaders to facilitate opportunities for meaningful participation and to acknowledge diverse contributions. Such a leadership stance mitigates the risk of power imbalances that can lead to disengagement or conflict, instead promoting a culture of openness, trust, and mutual respect. Applying Adler's theories to leadership behaviors involves a conscious effort to balance the inherent human drive for self-improvement with the responsibility to nurture a supportive and collaborative community. This balance is crucial in decision-making processes, where ethical considerations and the impact of decisions on team members and the wider community take precedence. Leaders are called upon to make choices that not only advance organizational objectives but also uphold principles of fairness, integrity, and social responsibility.

The integration of Adlerian concepts into leadership practices also necessitates a commitment to personal and organizational reflection and growth. Leaders must engage in ongoing self-examination and be open to feedback, using insights gained to refine their approach and better serve their teams and organizations. This reflective practice ensures that leadership is not static but evolves in response to new challenges, insights, and the changing needs of the organization and its people. Delving deeper into Adler's theories enriches our understanding of leadership, offering a framework for developing practices that are not only effective in achieving organizational goals but also ethical, inclusive, and socially responsible. By embracing the principles of striving for superiority, social interest, and community feeling, leaders can cultivate organizational cultures that are vibrant, resilient, and aligned with the broader aims of societal progress and well-being.

Developing a leadership style that harmonizes personal ambitions with the welfare of the group is crucial for fostering a collaborative and supportive environment. This balance is essential not only for the sustainable success of the organization but also for cultivating a workplace culture that values and nurtures its members. When leaders manage to strike this equilibrium, they create an atmosphere where mutual respect, shared goals, and collective achievement become the pillars upon which the organization stands.

The importance of this balanced leadership approach lies in its capacity to address the intrinsic human need for belonging and significance. Leaders who prioritize the welfare of the group over personal gain demonstrate a commitment to the well-being of their team members. This, in turn, cultivates trust and loyalty, as employees feel valued and understood, knowing that their contributions are recognized and that their welfare is a priority. Such an environment encourages team members to invest their best efforts, fostering a sense of ownership and dedication to the organization's objectives.

A leadership style that balances personal ambitions with group welfare inherently promotes collaboration. By valuing each team member's input and fostering an atmosphere where ideas can be shared freely, leaders encourage innovation and creative problem-solving. This collaborative spirit is crucial for navigating the complexities and challenges of the modern business landscape, where the collective intelligence and agility of the team often determine success.

This approach also has significant implications for ethical leadership and decision-making. Leaders who embody this balanced style are more likely to make decisions that consider the broader impact on their team, the organization, and even society at large. Ethical considerations become integral to the decision-making process, ensuring that actions taken are not only in pursuit of organizational goals but also align with values of fairness, integrity, and social responsibility.

Developing a leadership style that balances personal and group welfare requires a deep understanding of one's motivations, strengths, and areas for growth. It involves self-reflection and a willingness to engage in personal development, seeking feedback, and being open to change. This introspective process not only enhances the leader's effectiveness but also models a commitment to growth and learning that can inspire and motivate others. Leaders who succeed in balancing personal ambitions with the welfare of the group also excel in managing power dynamics within the organization. They use their influence to empower others, delegating authority and fostering leadership skills among their team members. This empowerment contributes to a more dynamic and resilient organization, where leadership is distributed, and team members are equipped to take on challenges and opportunities.

The development of a leadership style that balances personal ambitions with the welfare of the group is foundational to creating a collaborative, supportive, and ethical organizational culture. Such a leadership approach not only drives organizational success but also contributes to the personal and professional growth of team members. It creates a workplace where individuals are motivated to contribute their best, confident in the knowledge that their welfare is considered and valued. This balance is the hallmark of truly effective leadership, reflecting a deep understanding of the complex interplay between individual aspirations and the collective good.

**Managing Power Dynamics**

Navigating power dynamics effectively is a critical skill for leaders, and Adlerian principles offer valuable strategies for understanding and managing these dynamics within teams and organizations. Alfred Adler's theories, particularly his concepts of striving for superiority, social interest, and the importance of community feeling, provide a robust framework for leaders aiming to create a more collaborative, equitable, and motivated work environment. At the heart of Adler's approach is the recognition of the inherent desire in every individual to feel significant and to belong to a community. Leaders can harness this insight by fostering an environment where power is not hoarded but shared, where each team member's contributions are valued, and where the success of the group is prioritized over individual achievements. This approach not only democratizes power within the organization but also enhances team cohesion and collective efficacy.

One key strategy involves actively promoting social interest within the team. Leaders can achieve this by modeling empathy, cooperation, and concern for the well-being of others. By demonstrating how individual success is intertwined with the group's achievements, leaders can encourage team members to support one another, share knowledge, and work towards common goals. This creates a positive feedback loop where the team's success reinforces individual members' sense of belonging and significance.

Another important strategy is addressing feelings of inferiority and competition, which can exacerbate negative power dynamics. Leaders can mitigate these feelings by recognizing and celebrating each team member's unique strengths and contributions. Creating opportunities for individual development and emphasizing personal growth as a component of the team's success can help members see their personal advancement as aligned with, rather than in competition with, the achievements of their colleagues.

Effective communication is also crucial in navigating power dynamics. Leaders should strive for transparency in decision-making processes, actively solicit input from team members, and ensure that communication channels are open and accessible. This transparency helps to build trust, reduces the potential for misunderstanding and conflict, and empowers team members by giving them a voice in decisions that affect their work and the organization.

Leaders can use Adlerian principles to cultivate a culture of mutual respect and equality. By challenging traditional hierarchies and encouraging a more collaborative approach to leadership, leaders can break down barriers that perpetuate unhealthy power dynamics. This might involve implementing team-based decision-making, encouraging mentorship and peer support, and valuing contributions based on merit rather than position. Leaders also should engage in self-reflection and seek feedback on their leadership style and its impact on team dynamics. Understanding one's own motivations, biases, and behaviors is essential for identifying how one might unconsciously contribute to negative power dynamics. Leaders committed to personal growth and self-improvement set a powerful example for their teams, demonstrating that striving for superiority is a journey that encompasses not only professional achievements but also ethical conduct and interpersonal relationships.

Navigating power dynamics effectively requires leaders to apply Adlerian principles in a way that emphasizes social interest, fosters a sense of belonging and significance among team members, and promotes a culture of cooperation, respect, and mutual support. By doing so, leaders can transform power dynamics from a source of conflict and competition into a force for unity, innovation, and collective success.

Empathy, open communication, and mutual respect play pivotal roles in mitigating power imbalances and conflicts within teams and organizations. These elements foster an environment where all team members feel valued, understood, and empowered, which is essential for building trust, collaboration, and a positive organizational culture. Empathy is the ability to understand and share the feelings of another. In leadership, it involves recognizing the emotions, needs, and perspectives of team members. Empathetic leaders are adept at sensing undercurrents of dissatisfaction or disengagement that may signal underlying power imbalances or conflicts. By addressing these issues with sensitivity and care, leaders can prevent potential problems from escalating and ensure that all team members feel supported and heard. Empathy also allows leaders to tailor their approach to the unique motivations and concerns of individual team members, fostering a sense of personal connection and loyalty.

Open communication is crucial for breaking down barriers and promoting transparency within teams. It creates a platform for the expression of ideas, concerns, and feedback, making it easier to identify and address power imbalances and conflicts early on. Leaders who prioritize open communication encourage dialogue and dissent, demonstrating that they value diverse perspectives and are committed to fairness and inclusivity. This openness helps to demystify decision-making processes, reduce speculation and mistrust, and involve team members in shaping the direction and policies of the organization. As a result, team members are more likely to feel a sense of ownership and commitment to collective goals.

Mutual respect is the foundation upon which productive and positive relationships are built. When leaders show genuine respect for their team members' skills, contributions, and well-being, it sets a standard for interpersonal interactions within the team. Respectful leadership behaviors include acknowledging individual achievements, providing constructive feedback, and treating all team members equitably. This respect fosters a culture of appreciation and dignity, where power is not wielded as a tool of dominance but shared as a means of empowerment. Mutual respect also helps to smooth over conflicts, as team members feel that their viewpoints are valued and that differences can be resolved through dialogue rather than coercion.

Together, empathy, open communication, and mutual respect act as powerful antidotes to power imbalances and conflicts. They ensure that leadership is not about enforcing authority but about facilitating collaboration and growth. Leaders who embody these qualities can navigate the complexities of organizational life with grace, inspiring their teams to achieve their best while maintaining a harmonious and supportive work environment. In doing so, they not only enhance the effectiveness and resilience of their organizations but also contribute to a broader culture of empathy, openness, and respect in the business world.

**Fostering Collaborative Environments**

Creating collaborative environments that reflect Adlerian ideals involves cultivating spaces where the emphasis is placed on collective success over individual achievement. This approach, rooted in Alfred Adler's principles of social interest and community feeling, promotes a sense of belonging and significance among team members, fostering an atmosphere where collaboration and mutual support are paramount.

Adlerian psychology suggests that true fulfillment and success are achieved not through personal glorification but through contributions to the welfare of others. In the context of organizational leadership, this translates to fostering environments where the collective goals and achievements of the team are prioritized.

## Fostering a Sense of Belonging

One of the first steps in creating such an environment is to foster a strong sense of belonging and community within the team. Leaders can achieve this by ensuring that every team member feels valued and understood, recognizing that each individual brings unique strengths and perspectives to the table. Activities that promote team bonding and a shared sense of purpose, such as collaborative projects, team-building exercises, and open discussions about team goals and values, can enhance this sense of belonging.

## Encouraging Social Interest

Promoting social interest within teams means encouraging members to look beyond their personal ambitions and consider the broader impact of their work. Leaders can model this behavior by demonstrating a genuine concern for the well-being of team members, the community, and the environment. Highlighting the ways in which the team's work contributes to the greater good can also motivate individuals to adopt a more community-focused perspective.

## Cultivating Mutual Respect and Appreciation

Mutual respect and appreciation are critical in collaborative environments. Leaders can cultivate these values by acknowledging and celebrating the contributions of all team members, providing constructive feedback, and facilitating open and respectful communication. Recognizing the achievements of the team as a whole, rather than focusing solely on individual accomplishments, reinforces the importance of collective success.

## Practicing Democratic Leadership

Adopting a democratic leadership style allows for the distribution of power and decision-making across the team, ensuring that all voices are heard and considered. This approach aligns with Adlerian ideals by promoting equality and cooperation. Leaders can implement this by involving team members in setting goals, making decisions, and solving problems, thereby fostering a sense of ownership and shared responsibility for the team's success.

Creating Opportunities for Collaboration

Intentionally creating opportunities for collaboration is another way to emphasize collective success. This might involve structuring projects in a way that requires cross-functional teamwork, setting up mentorship and peer support systems, or organizing workshops and brainstorming sessions that encourage creative collaboration.

Addressing Conflicts Constructively

Constructive conflict resolution is essential in collaborative environments. Leaders should encourage open dialogue about disagreements and challenges, approaching conflicts as opportunities for growth and learning. By prioritizing the resolution of issues in a way that respects everyone's needs and contributions, leaders can maintain a cohesive and supportive team dynamic.

Creating collaborative environments that reflect Adlerian ideals involves a multifaceted approach centered on fostering community, promoting social interest, and emphasizing the importance of collective success. Leaders who successfully implement these strategies can cultivate teams that are not only more cohesive and productive but also more aligned with the principles of social responsibility and mutual support.

Leadership, according to Alfred Adler's principles, is fundamentally about nurturing an environment where team members feel a profound sense of belonging and are motivated to contribute meaningfully. This Adlerian approach emphasizes the critical role of leaders in fostering inclusive, supportive, and purpose-driven work cultures.

Creating a culture of belonging involves leaders taking active steps to ensure every team member feels included and valued. This goes beyond mere acceptance to celebrating the diversity of thoughts, backgrounds, and experiences within the team. Leaders who prioritize understanding and addressing individual needs affirm that everyone has a unique and valuable role to play. Such inclusivity strengthens interpersonal bonds and cultivates a sense of mutual respect and trust, laying the foundation for a cohesive team dynamic.

Encouraging contribution is also essential. Adler's idea of social interest—the innate desire to contribute to the welfare of others—suggests that people are most fulfilled when they feel their work serves a greater purpose. Leaders can tap into this drive by connecting team goals with wider social or organizational objectives, thereby imbuing daily tasks with deeper significance. Recognizing individual contributions to these collective goals reinforces a sense of purpose and belonging among team members.

Empowerment is another key element. By sharing responsibility and encouraging autonomy, leaders not only show trust in their team's capabilities but also enhance members' sense of ownership and commitment to their work. This empowerment fosters a proactive and collaborative environment where team members feel accountable to one another and dedicated to shared success.

Modeling social interest is crucial for leaders. Demonstrating genuine concern for the well-being of team members and the broader community sets a powerful example. Leaders who engage in acts of kindness, support community initiatives, or advocate for sustainable practices inspire their teams to adopt similar values of empathy and cooperation. This not only strengthens the team's internal dynamics but also positions the organization as a responsible and caring member of the wider community.

Addressing conflict with a community-focused approach is vital. Conflicts, when managed constructively, can strengthen rather than weaken team cohesion. Leaders adept in Adlerian principles approach disagreements with empathy, striving for resolutions that prioritize mutual understanding and the collective good. This method ensures that conflicts become opportunities for growth and learning, rather than sources of division.

Leadership inspired by Adlerian principles is transformative, guiding teams toward environments where belonging and contribution are not just encouraged but deeply embedded in the culture. Such leadership transcends the transactional aspects of work, creating spaces where individuals are motivated by a shared sense of purpose and commitment to the common good. Through inclusivity, empowerment, modeling social interest, and constructive conflict resolution, leaders can foster teams that are not only productive but also harmonious, resilient, and aligned with the broader aims of societal progress and well-being.

## Adler's Influence on Modern Leadership

Alfred Adler's psychological theories, particularly his emphasis on social interest, community feeling, and the importance of overcoming feelings of inferiority, have a profound and enduring relevance to contemporary leadership theories and practices. This is especially true for concepts like servant leadership and emotional intelligence, which have gained prominence in modern organizational contexts. Adler's ideas provide a foundational understanding of the psychological dynamics that underpin these leadership approaches, underscoring the importance of empathy, social contribution, and personal development in effective leadership.

Servant Leadership

Servant leadership, a term coined by Robert K. Greenleaf in the latter half of the 20th century, emphasizes the leader's role as primarily serving the needs of their team members. This approach aligns closely with Adler's concept of social interest, where the welfare of the group and the broader community takes precedence over individual ambitions. Servant leaders prioritize the growth and well-being of their team and the communities to which they belong, echoing Adler's ideas about the significance of contributing to the common good. In practice, this might involve fostering a supportive work environment, encouraging personal and professional development, and engaging in community service. Adler's emphasis on empathy and understanding also resonates with the servant leader's focus on listening to and understanding the needs of others, further highlighting the compatibility between Adlerian psychology and servant leadership principles.

Emotional Intelligence

The concept of emotional intelligence, popularized by Daniel Goleman in the 1990s, refers to the ability to recognize, understand, and manage one's own emotions and the emotions of others. Emotional intelligence is critical for effective leadership, as it influences communication, conflict resolution, and decision-making. Adler's insights into the importance of social interest and community feeling can be seen as early precursors to the principles of emotional intelligence. Understanding and managing one's emotions, particularly in the context of interpersonal relationships and group dynamics, is crucial for fostering a sense of belonging and community within teams. Leaders who exhibit high emotional intelligence are adept at navigating the complexities of human behavior, much like Adler advocated for an understanding of individual motivations and feelings of inferiority. By applying Adlerian principles, leaders can enhance their emotional intelligence, leading with empathy, fostering positive relationships, and creating a supportive and cohesive work environment.

Contemporary Relevance

The enduring relevance of Adler's ideas in contemporary leadership theories and practices underscores the timeless nature of his psychological insights. The parallels between Adlerian psychology, servant leadership, and emotional intelligence highlight a broader shift in leadership paradigms from hierarchical, authority-based models to more inclusive, empathetic, and people-centered approaches. This shift reflects a growing recognition of the importance of psychological well-being, social cohesion, and ethical responsibility in achieving organizational success.

In today's complex and rapidly changing organizational environments, the principles of servant leadership and emotional intelligence are more pertinent than ever. Leaders are challenged to navigate diverse and dispersed teams, address increasing societal expectations for corporate responsibility, and foster innovation and resilience in the face of constant change. Adler's emphasis on overcoming personal limitations, fostering social interest, and building community provides valuable guidance for leaders seeking to navigate these challenges effectively.

Adler's psychological theories offer profound insights into the nature of effective leadership, providing a foundation for contemporary approaches like servant leadership and emotional intelligence. By emphasizing empathy, social contribution, and personal growth, Adler's ideas continue to inspire leaders to strive for more compassionate, inclusive, and effective leadership practices.

Applying Adlerian concepts to leadership presents a unique set of challenges and opportunities, especially in today's diverse and rapidly evolving organizational contexts. Alfred Adler's emphasis on social interest, community feeling, and the importance of overcoming feelings of inferiority offers a rich framework for understanding and navigating the complexities of modern leadership.

One of the primary challenges in applying Adlerian principles to leadership is the inherent diversity within teams and organizations. Cultural, social, and personal differences among team members can make it difficult to foster a unified sense of community and social interest. Leaders must navigate these differences sensitively and skillfully, striving to create an inclusive environment where all team members feel valued and understood. This requires a deep understanding of individual and cultural dynamics, as well as the ability to adapt leadership styles to meet the varied needs and expectations of a diverse workforce.

Another challenge is the pace of change in contemporary organizational contexts. Rapid technological advancements, shifting market dynamics, and evolving societal expectations can strain the cohesion and stability of teams. Leaders must balance the need for innovation and adaptability with the maintenance of a stable and supportive community within the organization. Applying Adlerian concepts in such dynamic environments demands flexibility, foresight, and a commitment to fostering resilience and a shared sense of purpose among team members.

Despite these challenges, applying Adlerian concepts to leadership also presents significant opportunities. Adler's focus on social interest and the psychological well-being of individuals aligns well with contemporary values around corporate social responsibility, employee wellness, and ethical leadership. By embracing these principles, leaders can enhance their organization's social and environmental impact, attract and retain talent, and build a positive organizational reputation.

His emphasis on overcoming feelings of inferiority through personal and collective growth offers a powerful framework for leadership development. Leaders can use these insights to encourage continuous learning, foster a culture of feedback and self-improvement, and empower team members to take on challenges and develop their potential. This not only enhances individual and team performance but also contributes to a vibrant and innovative organizational culture.

Adlerian principles also provide a valuable perspective on conflict resolution and team dynamics. By understanding the underlying feelings of inferiority and striving for superiority that can drive conflict, leaders can address disputes more effectively, fostering a sense of belonging and mutual respect. This approach can strengthen team cohesion, enhance collaboration, and improve problem-solving and decision-making within the organization.

While applying Adlerian concepts to leadership in diverse and changing organizational contexts presents challenges, it also offers opportunities to foster more inclusive, adaptable, and socially responsible organizations. Leaders who navigate these challenges successfully can cultivate environments where team members feel valued and motivated to contribute to collective goals, driving organizational success and making a positive impact on society.

## Conclusion

Alfred Adler's exploration of human psychology offers profound insights into leadership and power dynamics, presenting a comprehensive framework that is as relevant today as it was in his time. His theory, centered on the interplay between the striving for superiority and the inherent need for social interest, provides a rich tapestry for understanding the motivations behind leadership actions and their impact on organizational life.

He introduced the concept that the drive for personal achievement, rooted in an attempt to overcome feelings of inferiority, is a fundamental human trait. This striving for superiority, when channeled appropriately by leaders, can lead to ambition and organizational success. However, he stressed the importance of balancing this drive with a genuine concern for the welfare of others. Effective leadership, according to Adler, is characterized by an ability to align personal and organizational goals with the broader aim of contributing positively to the community.

The significance of fostering a strong sense of community, or Gemeinschaftsgefühl, within teams and organizations is another cornerstone of Adler's theory. Leaders who cultivate environments where team members feel a sense of belonging and cooperation can effectively mitigate conflicts and power imbalances, leading to a more harmonious and productive workplace. This sense of community encourages collaboration, supports team cohesion, and enhances the collective capacity to achieve shared goals.

Adler's insights into power dynamics emphasize the need for leaders to be mindful of how their behaviors influence team dynamics and individual well-being. By prioritizing practices that encourage empathy, facilitate open communication, and demonstrate mutual respect, leaders can create inclusive spaces where power is equitably shared, and all members feel respected and valued.

Empowering team members is another critical aspect of Adlerian leadership. This empowerment involves encouraging autonomy, recognizing individual contributions, and supporting personal and professional growth, thereby fostering an environment ripe for innovation and shared success. He offers valuable strategies for resolving conflicts in ways that strengthen rather than weaken team relationships. Understanding the psychological underpinnings of conflicts allows leaders to address them constructively, promoting a culture of mutual respect and collaboration.

Applying Adlerian principles in the diverse and ever-changing landscape of modern organizations demands adaptability and a deep commitment to understanding and meeting the varied needs of team members. Leaders adept at navigating these complexities can leverage the strengths of a diverse workforce, driving innovation and adapting effectively to external challenges. Adler's emphasis on ethical leadership and decision-making highlights the importance of considering the broader implications of leadership actions. Leaders who integrate social interest into their decision-making processes are more likely to act ethically, make responsible decisions, and align their actions with the common good. Adler's contributions to the study of leadership and power dynamics advocate for a leadership approach that is compassionate, socially responsible, and deeply attuned to the psychological needs of individuals and teams. By balancing personal ambition with a commitment to the welfare of others and fostering an environment of empathy, inclusivity, and ethical integrity, leaders can inspire positive change and achieve sustainable organizational success.

Incorporating Adlerian concepts into leadership development holds transformative potential for creating environments where power is wielded constructively and collaboratively. Alfred Adler's psychological insights, especially his emphasis on social interest, community feeling, and the constructive management of power dynamics, provide a robust framework for redefining leadership in a way that promotes growth, unity, and positive change within organizations.

Adler's notion that true success and personal fulfillment arise from contributing to the welfare of others challenges traditional leadership models that prioritize hierarchical control and individual achievement. By shifting the focus towards social interest and the collective good, leaders can harness their power to create environments that foster mutual support, shared success, and a deep sense of belonging among team members. This Adlerian approach encourages leaders to view power not as a means of enforcing authority, but as a tool for empowering others, facilitating collaboration, and driving communal goals.

The transformative potential of integrating Adlerian principles into leadership development is particularly evident in the way it reorients leaders' perspectives on their roles and responsibilities. Leaders learn to appreciate the value of each team member's contributions, recognizing that the organization's strength lies in its diversity and collective capabilities. This understanding leads to more democratic and participatory leadership styles, where decision-making is shared, and team members are encouraged to take active roles in shaping their work environment and organizational direction.

His concepts offer valuable strategies for navigating and resolving conflicts in ways that enhance team cohesion rather than erode it. By understanding the underlying feelings of inferiority and striving for superiority that often fuel conflicts, leaders can address disputes with empathy and insight, fostering a culture where differences are resolved through constructive dialogue and mutual respect.

Incorporating Adlerian principles into leadership development also promotes emotional intelligence, a critical skill in managing interpersonal relationships and organizational dynamics. Leaders become more attuned to their own emotional responses and those of their team members, enabling them to communicate more effectively, manage stress and conflict, and build stronger, more resilient teams. His emphasis on community feeling and social interest aligns with contemporary values around corporate social responsibility and ethical leadership. Leaders who embody these Adlerian ideals are better positioned to guide their organizations towards practices that not only benefit the bottom line but also contribute positively to society and the environment.

The incorporation of Adlerian concepts into leadership development has the potential to fundamentally transform organizational cultures. By fostering environments where power is used constructively and collaboratively, leaders can cultivate workplaces characterized by empathy, inclusivity, and a shared commitment to the common good. This Adlerian approach to leadership not only enhances organizational effectiveness but also contributes to a more equitable, responsible, and compassionate society.

Leaders today are increasingly called upon to reflect deeply on their approaches to power and their capacity to foster a sense of community within their organizations. In light of Alfred Adler's concepts, this reflection is not just beneficial but essential for cultivating leadership practices that are balanced, socially interested, and ultimately more effective in today's complex organizational landscapes.

Power, in the Adlerian sense, should not be an end in itself but a means to achieve broader, community-oriented goals. Leaders are encouraged to examine their use of power critically: Is it being used to dominate and control, or to empower and uplift? Reflecting on this question can help leaders pivot towards a more constructive use of power, one that emphasizes empowerment, collaboration, and the facilitation of personal and professional growth among team members.

Cultivating a genuine sense of community feeling within an organization requires leaders to go beyond mere team-building activities. It involves creating a culture where every individual feels valued, understood, and connected to the collective mission of the organization. Leaders should ask themselves whether their actions and decisions reinforce this sense of belonging and shared purpose, or whether they inadvertently contribute to feelings of isolation or competition among team members.

Adler's emphasis on social interest as a cornerstone of healthy human functioning offers a powerful lens through which leaders can evaluate and enhance their leadership practices. Are the organization's goals aligned with the broader welfare of the community and society? Do leadership decisions consider the social and environmental impact? Reflecting on these questions can guide leaders toward a more socially responsible and ethically grounded approach to leadership.

Leaders are also encouraged to foster open dialogues within their teams about power dynamics, community feeling, and social interest. Such conversations can illuminate areas for improvement, reveal insights into the team's collective values and aspirations, and strengthen the bonds between team members and leaders. This open communication fosters a transparent and inclusive environment where power is shared, and collective success is prioritized.

In advocating for a more balanced and socially interested leadership practice, leaders are invited to embark on a journey of continuous self-improvement and reflection. This journey involves not only reassessing one's approach to power and community but also actively seeking feedback, engaging in lifelong learning, and embracing opportunities for personal and professional development.

Leadership that is guided by Adlerian principles of social interest and community feeling has the potential to transform organizations. By reflecting on and refining their approaches to power and community, leaders can build more cohesive, resilient, and purpose-driven teams. Such leadership not only achieves organizational objectives but also contributes to a more equitable, compassionate, and sustainable world.

# Chapter 3: Erik Erikson and Psychosocial Development in Leadership

Erik Erikson's theory of psychosocial development stands as a cornerstone in understanding human growth and the formation of identity through the lens of psychological and social challenges. Unlike theories that focus solely on the early years of life, Erikson's model spans the entire lifespan, delineating eight distinct stages from infancy to late adulthood. Each stage is characterized by a specific psychosocial crisis that individuals must navigate. The resolution of these crises, whether successful or not, profoundly influences personality development and behavior. Erikson's theory provides a valuable framework for exploring how these developmental stages impact leadership styles, capacities, and challenges.

In the realm of leadership, Erikson's stages offer insights into how leaders can evolve and mature through various life phases, each bringing its own set of challenges and growth opportunities. Understanding these stages can help leaders and those who develop leadership programs to appreciate the depth and complexity of leadership as a developmental journey. It highlights the importance of self-awareness, adaptability, and the continuous interplay between personal experiences and professional roles.

By applying Erikson's psychosocial development theory to leadership, we can explore the nuanced ways in which early experiences and subsequent psychosocial resolutions influence leadership behaviors, relationships, and effectiveness. This perspective encourages a more holistic approach to leadership development, one that considers the leader's entire life course, not just their professional experiences or skills. It underscores the significance of addressing and integrating personal growth challenges as part of enhancing one's capacity to lead others effectively.

Erikson's theory of psychosocial development profoundly illuminates the psychological foundations of leadership behavior and effectiveness, offering a nuanced view of how leaders grow and evolve through resolving life-stage crises. This developmental framework enriches our understanding of leadership beyond mere competencies, highlighting the interplay between an individual's psychological evolution and their leadership journey.

In the early stage of trust vs. mistrust, the development of trust emerges as a cornerstone of leadership. Leaders who effectively navigate this phase tend to excel in creating an atmosphere of trust within their teams, which is critical for fostering innovation and open communication. This foundational trust influences all subsequent interpersonal dynamics and leadership effectiveness. As individuals progress to the autonomy vs. shame and doubt stage, the emphasis shifts to developing self-confidence and independence. Leaders who successfully resolve this crisis display a remarkable ability to make autonomous decisions and inspire confidence in others, underpinning their capability to lead decisively and empower their team members to operate independently.

The initiative vs. guilt stage further refines a leader's approach, emphasizing the importance of taking proactive steps and assuming responsibility. This ability to initiate action and lead by example is crucial for motivating teams and driving organizational vision forward. Moving into the industry vs. inferiority phase, the focus on competence and mastery becomes paramount. Leaders who excel in this stage are not only deeply knowledgeable in their field but also committed to lifelong learning and the development of their team, enhancing both their credibility and the collective skills of their organization.

The transition through identity vs. role confusion is critical for cultivating authentic leadership. A strong and coherent sense of self enables leaders to navigate the complexities of their roles with integrity and clarity, ensuring their actions are aligned with their core values and vision. In the intimacy vs. isolation stage, the capacity to form deep and meaningful relationships is highlighted. Effective leadership is characterized by strong, trust-based connections with others, recognizing that the essence of leadership lies in the ability to influence and relate genuinely to people. The generativity vs. stagnation stage shifts the focus towards creating a lasting impact and mentoring the next generation. Leaders driven by a sense of generativity seek to leave a positive legacy, emphasizing the development of talent and the sustainability of their influence. Finally, the ego integrity vs. despair stage offers a reflective perspective on a leader's life and achievements, fostering a sense of fulfillment and wisdom. Leaders who reach this stage of development lead with a balanced and insightful approach, focusing on what truly matters over the long term.

Erikson's theory, therefore, provides a comprehensive lens through which to view the development of leadership. It highlights the importance of psychological growth throughout the lifespan in shaping effective, authentic, and visionary leaders. By integrating personal experiences and psychological development with professional roles, leaders can navigate the complexities of their roles with greater insight and empathy, ultimately enhancing their effectiveness and impact.

**Implications of Psychosocial Stages for Leadership**

Erikson's psychosocial stages offer a roadmap for understanding how various phases of personal development can influence and reflect in leadership qualities and challenges. Each stage, from infancy through late adulthood, contributes uniquely to the formation of a leader's identity, values, and approaches to challenges and relationships.

Infancy: Trust vs. Mistrust

In the infancy stage, the development of trust lays the foundation for future leadership qualities. Leaders who have successfully navigated this stage tend to exhibit a strong ability to build trust within their teams, crucial for creating a secure and open organizational culture. They are likely to be viewed as reliable and consistent, fostering an environment where team members feel safe to express ideas and take risks.

## Early Childhood: Autonomy vs. Shame and Doubt

The early childhood stage emphasizes autonomy and the development of a sense of self-control. Leaders shaped by positive experiences in this phase often display confidence in their decision-making and encourage independence within their teams. They balance providing guidance with empowering team members to take initiative, fostering a culture of accountability and self-reliance.

## Play Age: Initiative vs. Guilt

During the play age, the focus is on taking initiative and embracing leadership opportunities. Leaders who have effectively resolved the crisis of this stage are typically proactive, possess a strong sense of purpose, and are adept at motivating others. They are comfortable with leadership roles and use their initiative to drive innovation and progress within their organizations.

## School Age: Industry vs. Inferiority

This stage is crucial for developing a sense of competence and belief in one's abilities. Leaders who have mastered this stage tend to be diligent, resilient, and skilled in their fields. They value hard work and persistence, qualities they instill in their teams. Their leadership is characterized by a commitment to excellence and continuous improvement, inspiring their team members to develop their skills and strive for high standards.

## Adolescence: Identity vs. Role Confusion

Adolescence is a critical period for identity formation. Leaders who successfully navigate this stage have a clear sense of who they are and what they stand for, which is essential for authentic leadership. They possess a strong vision for their teams and organizations and are effective in communicating this vision, rallying their team members around shared goals and values.

Young Adulthood: Intimacy vs. Isolation

The ability to form intimate relationships and connect with others is developed during young adulthood. Leaders who excel in this stage are empathetic, possess strong interpersonal skills, and are capable of building deep, trusting relationships with their team members. They understand the importance of collaboration and are effective in creating a cohesive team environment.

Adulthood: Generativity vs. Stagnation

In adulthood, the focus shifts to generativity and the desire to contribute to the well-being of future generations. Leaders influenced by positive outcomes in this stage are visionary and focused on legacy. They prioritize mentoring, developing talent within their organizations, and implementing sustainable practices that ensure long-term success and impact.

Maturity: Ego Integrity vs. Despair

The final stage involves reflecting on one's life and contributions. Leaders who achieve ego integrity are wise, reflective, and possess a broad perspective. They are capable of guiding their organizations through challenges with insight and foresight, drawing on a lifetime of experiences. Their leadership is marked by a sense of calm and assurance, providing stability and confidence to their teams.

Erikson's psychosocial stages provide a valuable framework for understanding the depth and complexity of leadership development. Each stage contributes to the leader's approach to challenges, relationship-building, and overall effectiveness, highlighting the importance of ongoing personal development and self-awareness in leadership excellence.

The notion that unresolved issues in Erikson's earlier psychosocial stages can impact leadership style and effectiveness underscores the profound interconnection between personal development and professional leadership capabilities. Erikson's model suggests that each stage of development presents individuals with specific psychosocial crises that must be resolved to move forward healthily. When these issues remain unresolved, they can manifest in leadership behaviors, potentially hindering a leader's effectiveness and the overall health of the organization.

For instance, challenges in resolving the trust vs. mistrust crisis in infancy might result in leaders who struggle with trust—both in themselves and in others. Such leaders might find it difficult to delegate tasks, share power, or foster open communication within their teams, leading to a culture of micromanagement and mistrust that stifles innovation and team cohesion. Similarly, if individuals face difficulties in the autonomy vs. shame and doubt stage, they may emerge as leaders who either excessively control or, conversely, show indecisiveness. Their unresolved issues with autonomy can lead to either a dominating style that limits team empowerment or a lack of direction that leaves teams feeling unsupported and unclear about expectations.

In the initiative vs. guilt phase, unresolved issues can result in leaders who hesitate to take decisive action or, alternatively, take actions without considering their team's input or the broader implications. Such leaders might struggle with balancing assertiveness with inclusivity, potentially alienating team members or failing to harness the collective intelligence of their group. The industry vs. inferiority stage, when not navigated successfully, can lead to leaders who either overemphasize perfectionism and output, creating a high-pressure environment, or who lack confidence in their and their team's abilities, leading to low morale and underperformance.

At the heart of Erikson's adolescence stage, identity vs. role confusion, unresolved issues can manifest in leaders with a weak sense of self or vision, making it challenging to inspire or unify their teams. Leaders might struggle with authenticity, finding it difficult to align their personal values with their professional roles, leading to inconsistency and confusion among team members.

These examples illustrate how unresolved psychosocial issues can deeply affect leadership style and effectiveness, emphasizing the importance of self-awareness and personal development in leadership. Leaders who recognize and address these unresolved issues can enhance their leadership effectiveness, fostering healthier, more productive organizational cultures. This process might involve seeking feedback, engaging in reflective practices, or pursuing professional development and coaching opportunities aimed at resolving past conflicts and building stronger, more adaptive leadership capabilities.

Erikson's theory not only highlights the developmental underpinnings of effective leadership but also offers a pathway for growth and improvement. By acknowledging and working through unresolved issues from earlier psychosocial stages, leaders can unlock their full potential, leading to more effective, empathetic, and dynamic leadership practices that benefit both individuals and organizations.

**Early Stages: Trust vs. Mistrust and Autonomy vs. Shame**

Erikson's foundational stages, specifically those focusing on trust (trust vs. mistrust) and autonomy (autonomy vs. shame and doubt), lay the groundwork for developing the essential qualities of basic confidence and independence, which are critical for effective leadership. These stages are instrumental in shaping a leader's ability to establish trust within teams and foster an environment conducive to autonomous decision-making.

In the earliest stage of psychosocial development, the challenge of trust vs. mistrust revolves around the infant's basic needs being met by caregivers. Successful navigation of this stage results in a sense of trust, where the individual believes in the reliability and goodness of others and the world around them. For leaders, this foundational trust influences their ability to create and maintain trust within their teams. Leaders who have developed a strong sense of trust are more likely to be seen as reliable and consistent, qualities that encourage team members to feel secure, open, and willing to take risks. Trust is contagious; a leader who trusts their team members is more likely to be trusted in return. This reciprocal trust fosters a resilient team culture where challenges can be approached collaboratively and innovatively.

The stage of autonomy vs. shame and doubt focuses on the development of personal control and independence. As toddlers begin to assert their independence, successfully navigating this stage leads to a sense of autonomy. Leaders who have effectively resolved this crisis possess a strong sense of self-assurance and independence, allowing them to make confident decisions and encourage a similar sense of autonomy in their team members. Such leaders are adept at delegating tasks, empowering team members to take initiative, and supporting independent problem-solving efforts. This not only enhances the team's overall effectiveness but also contributes to each member's personal and professional growth. Conversely, unresolved issues in this stage might result in leaders who either micromanage, stifling team autonomy and innovation, or exhibit indecisiveness, undermining their authority and the team's direction.

The successful resolution of these foundational stages has a profound impact on a leader's effectiveness. Trust and autonomy are not just personal traits but are also reflected in a leader's approach to managing teams. Leaders grounded in trust and autonomy are more likely to:

- Establish a culture of open communication and mutual respect, where team members feel valued and understood.

- Encourage risk-taking within a supportive framework, where failures are seen as opportunities for learning rather than occasions for blame.

- Delegate effectively, recognizing and utilizing the strengths of each team member, thereby fostering a sense of ownership and responsibility.
- Create an environment where autonomous decision-making is encouraged, leading to higher levels of innovation and team satisfaction.

Erikson's stages of trust and autonomy are not merely steps in individual development but are also crucial in cultivating the qualities necessary for transformative leadership. By understanding the significance of these stages, leaders can reflect on their own developmental journey, recognizing areas of strength and opportunities for growth. In doing so, they can enhance their ability to build trustful relationships, empower their teams, and lead more effectively in an ever-changing organizational landscape.

**Middle Stages: Initiative vs. Guilt and Industry vs. Inferiority**

The middle stages of Erikson's psychosocial development, initiative vs. guilt and industry vs. inferiority, are critical periods where the qualities of initiative and industry are cultivated. These stages significantly influence leadership qualities such as innovation, motivation, and the capacity for hard work. Understanding and integrating the lessons from these stages can help leaders enhance their effectiveness and foster these essential qualities within their teams.

In the initiative vs. guilt stage, children learn to assert power and control through directing play and other social interactions. Successfully navigating this stage fosters a sense of initiative, allowing individuals to take actions that influence their environment positively. For leaders, this translates into the courage to innovate, take calculated risks, and inspire action within their organizations. Leaders who have mastered the art of taking initiative are adept at identifying opportunities, proposing novel solutions, and motivating their teams to embrace change and tackle challenges.

To cultivate initiative within themselves and their teams, leaders can:

- Encourage experimentation and support team members in taking calculated risks, emphasizing that failure is a valuable part of learning and growth.

- Create opportunities for team members to lead projects or initiatives, thereby developing their leadership skills and sense of agency.

- Model initiative by actively seeking out new ideas, staying informed about industry trends, and being open to change and innovation.

The industry vs. inferiority stage is where individuals learn to be industrious through consistent effort and a sense of accomplishment in their skills and tasks. Successfully resolving this crisis builds a foundation for a strong work ethic, perseverance, and pride in one's accomplishments. In a leadership context, this stage underlines the importance of hard work, dedication, and the pursuit of excellence. Leaders who value industry are not only committed to their personal and professional development but also strive to instill these qualities in their teams.

To foster a sense of industry and a strong work ethic within their teams, leaders can:

- Recognize and celebrate hard work and achievements, making sure team members feel valued for their contributions.

- Set clear, achievable goals that challenge the team while also providing the resources and support needed to attain them.

- Encourage a culture of continuous learning and improvement, where team members are motivated to develop new skills and refine existing ones.

By focusing on the development of initiative and industry, leaders can create dynamic, motivated teams capable of innovative thinking and sustained effort towards achieving organizational goals. Cultivating these qualities requires a supportive environment where taking initiative is rewarded, and hard work is recognized and celebrated. Leaders play a pivotal role in creating such an environment, demonstrating through their actions the value of initiative and industry. Through strategic encouragement, recognition, and role modeling, leaders can significantly impact their teams' ability to innovate, stay motivated, and work hard towards collective success.

## Adolescence to Young Adulthood: Identity vs. Role Confusion and Intimacy vs. Isolation

The transition from adolescence to young adulthood in Erikson's psychosocial stages—identity vs. role confusion and intimacy vs. isolation—presents pivotal challenges and opportunities for leadership development. These stages are crucial for leadership identity formation and the ability to forge close, trusting relationships within professional contexts. Successfully navigating these challenges can significantly enhance leadership authenticity and team cohesion.

This stage focuses on the development of a coherent sense of self, including one's values, beliefs, and goals. For leaders, this stage is foundational to developing a strong leadership identity. A well-defined sense of identity enables leaders to act with conviction, maintain consistency in decision-making, and communicate their vision effectively. Leaders with a strong sense of self are more likely to be perceived as authentic and credible, inspiring confidence and trust among their team members.

To navigate this stage successfully, leaders can:

- Engage in self-reflection to clarify their values, strengths, and weaknesses, and understand how these influence their leadership style.

- Seek feedback from mentors, peers, and team members to gain diverse perspectives on their leadership approach and areas for growth.

- Commit to lifelong learning, embracing opportunities to expand their understanding of themselves and the world around them, thereby refining their leadership identity.

In young adulthood, the challenge shifts to developing intimate, meaningful relationships while avoiding feelings of isolation. For leaders, this stage underscores the importance of building deep, trusting connections with team members and colleagues. Such relationships are essential for fostering open communication, collaboration, and a strong team dynamic. Leaders who excel in creating a sense of intimacy within their teams are better equipped to navigate conflicts, motivate team members, and cultivate a supportive work environment.

Strategies for leaders to enhance intimacy and trust within their teams include:

- Demonstrating vulnerability by sharing their own experiences, challenges, and learnings, thereby encouraging others to do the same.

- Investing time in getting to know team members on a personal level, showing genuine interest in their well-being and professional development.

- Creating a culture of openness and psychological safety, where team members feel comfortable expressing their ideas, concerns, and feedback without fear of judgment or retribution.

Successfully navigating the stages of identity and intimacy equips leaders with the authenticity and relational skills necessary for effective leadership. Leaders who are secure in their identity can lead with authenticity, aligning their actions with their values and vision. Simultaneously, those who have developed the capacity for close relationships are more adept at building cohesive, resilient teams based on trust and mutual respect.

The challenges of identity and intimacy are not merely personal milestones but are integral to developing the depth and authenticity required for impactful leadership. By embracing these developmental tasks, leaders can enhance their effectiveness, foster stronger team connections, and create a work environment characterized by trust, respect, and shared purpose.

### Adulthood: Generativity vs. Stagnation

In adulthood, the psychosocial stage of generativity vs. stagnation becomes a focal point, with significant implications for leadership. Erikson defined generativity as the concern for establishing and guiding the next generation, encompassing not only parenthood but also productivity and creativity in a broader sense. For leaders, this stage underscores the importance of nurturing talent, fostering innovation, and contributing to the organization's legacy. A strong sense of generativity influences a leader's approach to mentorship, their drive for innovation, and their capacity to lead organizational change effectively.

Leaders who prioritize generativity are actively involved in mentoring and developing their team members. They see their role not merely as managers but as cultivators of talent, investing time and resources in training programs, professional development opportunities, and one-on-one coaching. This commitment to the growth of others not only enhances the skills and capabilities within the organization but also strengthens the bond between leaders and their teams, fostering a culture of continuous learning and mutual support.

Generativity also fuels a leader's drive for innovation. Leaders with a generative mindset are continually looking for ways to improve, innovate, and push the boundaries of what's possible. They encourage creative thinking and experimentation within their teams, viewing failures as valuable learning experiences.

This openness to new ideas and willingness to take calculated risks are crucial for driving organizational change and staying competitive in an ever-evolving business landscape.

A sense of generativity is essential for leading organizational change. Leaders who are motivated by a desire to leave a lasting positive impact on their organization are more likely to initiate and sustain change efforts. They are adept at articulating a compelling vision for the future, one that resonates with their team members and aligns with the organization's values and goals. By engaging and inspiring their teams, these leaders can mobilize collective action towards achieving transformative goals, ensuring that the organization remains adaptable and resilient in the face of challenges.

The stage of generativity vs. stagnation offers a valuable lens through which to view leadership. Leaders who embrace generativity are not only focused on achieving immediate goals but are also deeply committed to the long-term well-being and success of their organization and its people. They understand that their legacy is defined not just by what they accomplish but by the impact they have on others and the foundation they lay for future generations. By fostering a culture of mentorship, innovation, and change, generative leaders play a pivotal role in shaping the future of their organizations, making a lasting contribution that extends far beyond their tenure.

**Later Stages: Ego Integrity vs. Despair**

In the later stage of Erikson's psychosocial development, ego integrity vs. despair, individuals reflect on their lives and careers, grappling with whether they have lived meaningfully and made significant contributions. This stage holds profound implications for senior leaders as they consider their legacies, achievements, and the process of transitioning, including succession planning and retirement. Successfully navigating this stage fosters a sense of ego integrity, enabling leaders to look back on their lives with a sense of fulfillment and wisdom, whereas failure leads to feelings of despair and regret.

For senior leaders, this reflective process is not just a personal journey but also influences their professional actions and decisions, particularly in shaping their legacy within the organization. Leaders who achieve ego integrity are characterized by their wisdom, a deep understanding borne of experience, successes, and failures. This wisdom is invaluable in guiding organizations through change, mentoring the next generation of leaders, and making strategic decisions that will impact the organization's future.

Wisdom and integrity also play a crucial role in succession planning. Leaders who have reached this stage of development understand the importance of ensuring that the organization can thrive beyond their tenure. They invest time in identifying and developing potential successors, imparting their knowledge, and gradually handing over responsibilities in a way that ensures a smooth transition. This process is guided by a desire to leave the organization in capable hands, ensuring its continued success and sustainability.

Leaders in the ego integrity stage often focus on solidifying their legacy, not through personal accolades but through the lasting impact of their work on the organization and its people. They may initiate projects or policies that embody their values and vision, aiming to instill a culture that will endure. Their approach to leadership becomes more about stewarding the organization's mission and ensuring its alignment with core values.

Retirement, therefore, is seen not as an end but as a transition—a handing over of the baton to the next generation. Leaders at this stage approach retirement with a sense of peace and satisfaction, knowing they have contributed to building something lasting. They remain available as mentors and advisors, offering their wisdom without clinging to power, thereby facilitating new leadership's growth and development.

The stage of ego integrity vs. despair offers senior leaders an opportunity to reflect on their careers and life achievements, emphasizing the importance of wisdom, integrity, and a forward-looking perspective in shaping their legacy. By focusing on meaningful contributions, effective succession planning, and the long-term well-being of the organization, leaders can ensure that their impact endures, marking a leadership journey characterized by depth, purpose, and a commitment to the greater good.

**Strategies for Navigating Psychosocial Development in Leadership**

Engaging with and resolving the crises characteristic of Erikson's psychosocial stages can significantly enhance a leader's development and effectiveness. Here are practical strategies for leaders at various stages of psychosocial development:

Trust vs. Mistrust

- Build Trust Within Yourself and Others: Cultivate self-trust by honoring your commitments and being consistent in your actions. Extend this trust to your team by demonstrating reliability, openness, and fairness in all interactions.

- Create a Trusting Environment: Foster a culture where team members feel safe to share ideas and take risks. Encourage open communication and show vulnerability as a leader to strengthen trust within the team.

Autonomy vs. Shame and Doubt

- Encourage Independence: Empower your team members by delegating tasks and allowing them the autonomy to complete projects in their own way. This builds their confidence and your trust in their capabilities.

- Promote a Culture of Learning: Create opportunities for professional development that enable team members to grow their skills and independence. Celebrate successes and view mistakes as learning opportunities.

## Initiative vs. Guilt

- Foster Initiative: Encourage team members to take the lead on projects and to propose new ideas. Create an environment where initiative is rewarded and where team members feel their contributions are valued.

- Balance Action with Reflection: Teach your team to reflect on their actions and outcomes. This helps them understand the impact of their initiatives and how to balance enthusiasm with practical considerations.

## Industry vs. Inferiority

- Cultivate a Strong Work Ethic: Model diligence, perseverance, and a commitment to quality. Encourage these traits in your team by setting high but achievable standards and recognizing hard work and achievements.

- Support Skill Development: Invest in training and resources that help team members develop their industry knowledge and competencies. This not only enhances team performance but also boosts individual self-esteem and a sense of mastery.

## Identity vs. Role Confusion

- Clarify Personal and Professional Identity: Engage in self-reflection to understand your core values and leadership philosophy. Share these with your team to foster a sense of shared identity and purpose.

- Encourage Exploration: Support team members in exploring different roles and projects that help them refine their professional identities. This can strengthen their commitment and alignment with organizational goals.

## Intimacy vs. Isolation

- Build Meaningful Relationships: Invest time in developing deep, trusting relationships with team members. Show genuine interest in their well-being and professional growth.

- Promote Team Cohesion: Facilitate team-building activities and opportunities for team members to connect on a personal level. This strengthens interpersonal relationships and reduces feelings of isolation.

Generativity vs. Stagnation

- Mentor the Next Generation: Actively mentor and develop emerging leaders within your organization. Share your knowledge and experiences to guide them in their growth.

- Contribute to the Organization's Legacy: Initiate projects or policies that have a lasting positive impact on the organization and its culture. Focus on creating a legacy that aligns with your values and the organization's mission.

Ego Integrity vs. Despair

- Reflect on Your Leadership Journey: Take time to reflect on your achievements and challenges. Share these reflections with others as lessons learned and as a way to document your leadership legacy.

- Plan for Succession: Engage in succession planning to ensure the organization continues to thrive. Mentor potential successors and gradually transfer knowledge and responsibilities to ensure a smooth transition.

By actively engaging with the challenges of each psychosocial stage, leaders can foster their own development and enhance their effectiveness. These strategies not only contribute to personal growth but also to the cultivation of high-performing, resilient teams and organizations.

The journey through Erikson's psychosocial stages underscores the critical importance of self-awareness, reflective practice, and seeking feedback in navigating one's developmental challenges. These processes are essential for leaders aiming to enhance their leadership effectiveness and personal growth, as they provide the insights and perspectives necessary to understand and address underlying issues impacting their leadership style and behavior.

Self-Awareness

Self-awareness is the foundation upon which leaders can build an understanding of their own psychosocial development. It involves a deep, honest examination of one's strengths, weaknesses, emotional triggers, values, and the unresolved issues from earlier developmental stages that may influence current behavior and decision-making. For leaders, cultivating self-awareness means recognizing how their experiences across the psychosocial stages affect their approach to leadership, including how they build trust, assert autonomy, take initiative, and foster relationships. By achieving a higher level of self-awareness, leaders can identify areas for personal growth and development that align with their desired leadership identity and effectiveness.

Reflective Practice

Reflective practice complements self-awareness by offering a structured approach to understanding one's experiences, behaviors, and emotions. This involves regularly taking time to reflect on actions taken, decisions made, and their outcomes. Reflection allows leaders to consider the impact of their leadership style on their team and organization, evaluate the alignment of their actions with their values and goals, and assess their progress in resolving developmental challenges. Through reflective practice, leaders can gain insights into their leadership dynamics, identify patterns that may be holding them back, and uncover new strategies for personal and professional growth.

Seeking Feedback

Feedback from peers, mentors, team members, and other stakeholders is invaluable in providing leaders with external perspectives on their leadership style and effectiveness. Seeking and being open to feedback can illuminate blind spots in self-perception and highlight areas of developmental need that may not be apparent through self-reflection alone. Constructive feedback offers concrete information on how a leader's behavior is perceived and the impact it has on others, facilitating targeted improvements. Engaging in regular feedback sessions encourages a culture of continuous learning and adaptation, both for the leader and the organization.

Navigating one's developmental challenges through self-awareness, reflective practice, and seeking feedback is a dynamic and ongoing process. It requires commitment, openness to change, and a willingness to confront and work through uncomfortable truths. However, the benefits of engaging in these practices are profound. Leaders who are self-aware, reflective, and receptive to feedback are better equipped to address their developmental needs, lead with greater authenticity and effectiveness, and foster healthy, resilient teams and organizations. Ultimately, these practices not only enhance leadership capabilities but also contribute to a fulfilling and meaningful leadership journey.

**Psychosocial Development and Leadership Effectiveness**

Erikson's stages of psychosocial development provide a comprehensive framework for understanding the complexities of human growth and how this influences leadership. A deep understanding of one's journey through these stages can significantly enhance leadership qualities, including integrity, wisdom, and generativity, by offering insights into the psychological underpinnings of behaviors, motivations, and interpersonal dynamics.

Starting from the foundational stages of trust vs. mistrust and autonomy vs. shame, leaders learn the importance of building trust within themselves and their teams and fostering an environment that encourages independence and self-assurance. These early stages set the groundwork for a leader's ability to create a secure, empowering atmosphere that is crucial for innovative and autonomous team action.

As leaders progress through the stages of initiative vs. guilt and industry vs. inferiority, they develop the courage to innovate and the dedication to pursue excellence. Successfully navigating these challenges fosters a proactive mindset and a strong work ethic, qualities that are indispensable for effective leadership. These stages encourage leaders to take calculated risks, motivate their teams, and commit to lifelong learning and skill development.

The crucial stages of identity vs. role confusion and intimacy vs. isolation are instrumental in forming a leader's sense of self and ability to form close, meaningful relationships. A well-defined identity enables leaders to lead with authenticity and clarity, inspiring trust and loyalty among team members. Simultaneously, the capacity for intimacy ensures that leaders can cultivate strong bonds within their teams, essential for collaboration and mutual support.

In adulthood, the stage of generativity vs. stagnation highlights the importance of mentoring and contributing to the organization's legacy. Leaders who embrace generativity focus on nurturing the next generation, driving innovation, and leading change with a long-term perspective. This stage emphasizes the leader's role in shaping the future, not just through personal achievements but through the lasting impact of their contributions to others and the organization.

The later stage of ego integrity vs. despair offers leaders a reflective vantage point to assess their careers and life achievements. Achieving ego integrity brings a sense of fulfillment and wisdom, qualities that allow leaders to guide their organizations with insight and foresight. It underscores the importance of reflection in cultivating a leadership approach marked by integrity, wisdom, and a deep understanding of the human experience.

Synthesizing the insights gained from Erikson's stages reveals that a profound understanding of one's psychosocial development can lead to enhanced leadership qualities. Leaders who engage deeply with their developmental journey are better equipped to lead with integrity, embody wisdom in their decision-making, and demonstrate generativity in their approach to leadership. This depth of understanding and personal growth not only enhances their effectiveness as leaders but also contributes to building healthier, more resilient organizations.

Below are some hypothetical case examples that illustrate how successfully navigating specific psychosocial stages can lead to profound personal growth and markedly improved leadership outcomes. By addressing and resolving developmental challenges, leaders can unlock their full potential, fostering environments that are more trusting, innovative, and aligned with their authentic selves and values.

Case Example 1: Trust vs. Mistrust - Building a Culture of Trust

Maria, a seasoned CEO, recognized early in her career that her difficulty in trusting her team stemmed from unresolved issues in the trust vs. mistrust stage. Despite her team's competence, Maria found herself micromanaging, fearing that without her direct oversight, projects would fail. Acknowledging this issue, she embarked on a journey of self-reflection and sought mentorship to understand the roots of her mistrust. Through this process, Maria learned to build trust in herself and others, gradually delegating more responsibilities and empowering her team. As a result, not only did her organization thrive due to increased innovation and team autonomy, but Maria also developed a deeper sense of trust in her relationships, fostering a culture where team members felt valued and empowered.

Case Example 2: Autonomy vs. Shame and Doubt - Fostering Independence

Alex, a technology startup founder, struggled with indecisiveness and a lack of confidence in his leadership, rooted in unresolved autonomy vs. shame and doubt issues. Recognizing that this was hampering his company's growth and stifling his team's creative potential, Alex sought coaching to work through these challenges. By consciously taking steps to affirm his decision-making capabilities and encouraging team members to take on leadership roles within projects, Alex not only bolstered his self-esteem but also cultivated a more dynamic and innovative team environment. This shift led to a significant turnaround in the startup's fortunes, with improved team morale, faster decision-making, and a string of successful product launches.

Case Example 3: Generativity vs. Stagnation - Leaving a Lasting Legacy

Samantha, a senior executive at a multinational corporation, found herself contemplating her legacy as she approached retirement. Recognizing the importance of the generativity vs. stagnation stage, she focused on mentoring young leaders within the organization, sharing her knowledge and experiences to prepare them for future challenges. Samantha initiated a leadership development program that not only addressed technical skills but also emphasized the importance of ethical leadership and social responsibility. Her efforts resulted in a new generation of leaders who were well-equipped to guide the organization into the future. Samantha retired knowing she had contributed to a lasting legacy that would benefit the organization and its stakeholders for years to come.

Case Example 4: Identity vs. Role Confusion - Cultivating Authentic Leadership

Jordan, the head of a non-profit organization, faced a crisis of identity, feeling caught between personal values and the expectations of the role. This dissonance led to a lack of fulfillment and effectiveness as a leader. Through introspection and professional development focused on aligning personal and organizational values, Jordan underwent a transformative journey. By embracing an authentic leadership style, Jordan was able to inspire the team with a renewed sense of purpose and vision that resonated deeply with personal and organizational values. This authenticity led to increased engagement from both the team and the broader community, significantly advancing the organization's mission.

## Conclusion

Erik Erikson's theory of psychosocial development offers a rich framework for understanding the complexities of leadership development through the lens of eight distinct stages that span from infancy to late adulthood. His contributions shed light on how each stage, characterized by specific crises and challenges, plays a crucial role in shaping an individual's capacity for leadership, their interpersonal relationships, and their ability to navigate the demands of leadership roles.

His initial stages emphasize the importance of trust, autonomy, initiative, and industry in laying the foundation for effective leadership. These early experiences influence a leader's ability to build trust within teams, foster independence and creativity, and cultivate a strong work ethic and competence. As individuals progress through these stages, they develop the essential qualities of confidence, self-reliance, and a proactive approach to challenges—traits that are indispensable for inspiring and guiding others. The middle stages of Erikson's framework, focusing on identity and intimacy, are pivotal for leadership identity formation and the development of meaningful, trust-based relationships within professional contexts. Successfully navigating these stages allows leaders to lead with authenticity, clearly communicate their vision, and build cohesive, collaborative teams. These stages underscore the importance of self-awareness and the capacity for deep, interpersonal connections in effective leadership.

In adulthood, the challenge of generativity versus stagnation becomes central, highlighting the significance of mentoring, innovation, and legacy within leadership. Leaders who embrace generativity focus on nurturing talent, driving organizational change, and ensuring that their contributions have a lasting positive impact. This stage emphasizes the leader's role in shaping the future and the value of a long-term perspective that prioritizes the growth and success of others and the organization as a whole.

Finally, the later stage of ego integrity versus despair offers leaders a reflective vantage point from which to assess their careers and contributions. Achieving ego integrity brings a sense of fulfillment and wisdom, allowing leaders to guide with insight, balance, and a focus on what truly matters. It underscores the importance of a reflective approach to leadership, characterized by integrity, wisdom, and a consideration of one's legacy.

Erikson's contributions to the understanding of psychosocial aspects of leadership development highlight the deep interconnection between personal growth and professional leadership capabilities. By examining leadership development through the stages of psychosocial development, Erikson provides a comprehensive view of the psychological challenges and opportunities that shape effective, authentic, and impactful leaders. His theory encourages a holistic approach to leadership development, one that recognizes the importance of continuous personal and professional growth and the integration of life experiences into leadership practices.

Erikson's theory of psychosocial development underscores the profound impact of personal growth on leadership effectiveness. Engaging with one's own developmental journey is crucial for leaders aiming to foster authenticity, emotional intelligence, and effectiveness in their leadership style. This engagement requires leaders to reflect deeply on their experiences at each stage of development, understanding how these experiences have shaped their values, behaviors, and approaches to leadership. The process of introspection and self-discovery enables leaders to identify and address any unresolved issues that may hinder their leadership. By resolving these issues, leaders can develop a stronger sense of self, which is essential for authentic leadership. Authentic leaders are genuine, transparent, and consistent in their actions and decisions, inspiring trust and loyalty among their followers. They are able to communicate their vision and values clearly, motivating their teams towards shared goals.

Emotional intelligence, a key component of effective leadership, is deeply rooted in an understanding of one's own emotions and the emotions of others. Leaders who are attuned to their developmental experiences are better equipped to manage their emotions, empathize with team members, and navigate complex interpersonal dynamics. This emotional awareness facilitates strong, meaningful connections with others, enhancing team cohesion and collaboration.

Engaging with one's developmental journey also promotes a leadership style that is adaptable and responsive to change. Leaders who are self-aware and reflective are more open to learning and growth, enabling them to adjust their leadership approach as needed to meet the evolving needs of their team and organization. They are able to embrace challenges as opportunities for development, fostering a culture of resilience and continuous improvement.

Leaders who are committed to their own personal development are more likely to prioritize the development of their team members. They recognize the value of mentoring and supporting others in their growth, contributing to the development of the next generation of leaders. This generative approach not only enhances the capabilities of the team but also leaves a lasting positive impact on the organization.

Engaging with one's own developmental journey is essential for leaders seeking to cultivate a leadership style that is authentic, emotionally intelligent, and effective. By reflecting on and integrating their experiences across Erikson's psychosocial stages, leaders can unlock their full potential, fostering environments that are more inclusive, innovative, and aligned with their core values. This commitment to personal and professional growth not only benefits the leader but also has a profound positive influence on their team and organization.

Erikson's work on psychosocial development provides a comprehensive framework for understanding the continuous process of growth that profoundly shapes a leader's approach to their role and their legacy within their organizations. Leaders are encouraged to view their developmental journey not as a series of past events but as an ongoing process that influences their behavior, decision-making, and interpersonal relationships. By reflecting on how each stage of psychosocial development has impacted them, leaders can gain valuable insights into their leadership style, strengths, weaknesses, and areas for further growth.

Understanding the nuances of one's own development emphasizes the importance of self-awareness in leadership. It allows leaders to recognize the origins of their motivations, fears, and patterns of interaction with others. Such awareness can lead to more authentic leadership, as leaders align their actions with their core values and beliefs, thereby inspiring trust and respect among their team members. This alignment between personal values and professional conduct also contributes to a leader's legacy, defining how they are remembered and the impact they leave on their organization.

Reflecting on psychosocial development also enhances a leader's emotional intelligence. By acknowledging and working through unresolved issues from earlier stages, leaders can better manage their emotions and empathize with others. This emotional agility is crucial for building strong relationships, navigating conflict, and fostering a supportive and inclusive team environment. Leaders who engage with their developmental journey are better positioned to mentor and develop others. Understanding their own growth process enables them to recognize and nurture the potential in their team members, guiding them through their challenges and supporting their professional development. This generative approach not only enhances team capabilities but also contributes to the sustainability and success of the organization.

Leaders are also encouraged to view their psychosocial development in the context of their legacy. By considering how they want to be remembered and the impact they wish to have, leaders can make more deliberate choices about their behavior, priorities, and the culture they cultivate. This forward-looking perspective helps ensure that their leadership not only meets the immediate needs of their team and organization but also contributes to long-term well-being and growth.

Erikson's theory of psychosocial development offers leaders a valuable lens through which to view their personal and professional growth. By reflecting on their own developmental journey as a continuous process, leaders can enhance their self-awareness, emotional intelligence, and ability to positively influence others. This reflective practice not only improves leadership effectiveness but also shapes a leader's approach to their role and their lasting legacy within their organizations. Leaders are thus encouraged to embrace this journey, continuously striving for growth and understanding to achieve their fullest potential as individuals and as leaders.

# Chapter 4: Wilfred Bion and Group Dynamics

Wilfred Bion, a distinguished figure in the field of psychoanalysis, made seminal contributions that extended the understanding of group dynamics and the intricate unconscious processes that underpin them. His work, deeply rooted in psychoanalytic principles, offers profound insights into how groups operate at both conscious and unconscious levels. Bion's exploration into the psychological underpinnings of group behavior has provided a robust framework for analyzing, interpreting, and influencing group dynamics in various contexts, including organizational leadership and team management. His background, marked by his experiences in the military and later in clinical settings, significantly informed his theories. His observations of group behavior, particularly under stress, led him to develop the basic assumption theory, a concept that elucidates the underlying, often unspoken, assumptions that guide group interactions. According to Bion, groups tend to operate under three basic assumptions—dependency, fight-flight, and pairing—each of which emerges in response to the group's unmet needs and desires.

The introduction of Bion's basic assumption theory into the discourse on group dynamics has been transformative, offering leaders and practitioners a lens through which to view the often complex and irrational behaviors that groups can exhibit. Understanding these basic assumptions enables leaders to better manage group dynamics, facilitating more effective communication, decision-making, and problem-solving within teams.

Bion's insights into the role of unconscious processes in group behavior have profound implications for leadership. They suggest that leaders must be attuned not only to the explicit goals and tasks of the group but also to the underlying emotional and psychological currents that influence group behavior. By applying Bion's theories, leaders can navigate the challenges of group dynamics with greater awareness and finesse, fostering a more cohesive, adaptive, and productive team environment.

In this chapter, we delve into Wilfred Bion's contributions to our understanding of group dynamics, examining how his theories can be applied to enhance leadership effectiveness and team performance. Through an exploration of basic assumption theory and its relevance to contemporary leadership challenges, we aim to equip leaders with the tools and insights needed to harness the power of group dynamics for organizational success.

**Bion's Basic Assumption Theory**

Wilfred Bion's Basic Assumption Theory is a cornerstone of his work on group dynamics, offering insights into the unconscious processes that underpin group behavior. Bion proposed that groups unconsciously operate according to one of three basic assumptions—dependency, fight-flight, and pairing. These assumptions influence the group's behavior, often bypassing rational decision-making processes to satisfy deeper, instinctual needs.

Dependency

This assumption posits that group members behave as if they are dependent on a leader or an external entity to provide security, direction, and sustenance. In a dependency mode, the group looks to the leader to solve its problems, make decisions, and provide a sense of safety. This can manifest in groups that exhibit a lack of initiative, passivity, or an overreliance on the leader for guidance and approval. Leaders may find that such groups demand constant reassurance and direction, showing little capacity for autonomous action or problem-solving.

Fight-Flight

Under the fight-flight assumption, groups operate as if they must either confront or flee from a perceived threat. This assumption is characterized by behaviors geared towards attacking the threat or evading it. In a group dynamic, this may present as aggression towards competitors or other teams, conflict within the group, or a tendency to avoid addressing difficult issues directly. Leaders of such groups might observe a heightened sense of urgency, conflict, or a predisposition to disengage from challenges rather than seeking constructive solutions.

Pairing

The pairing assumption is based on the group's unconscious belief that salvation or resolution of its issues will come from the emergence of a pair of members who will produce a creative solution or a new leader. This assumption often manifests in groups through a focus on potential relationships or alliances within the group that are idealized to bring about positive change. It can lead to a sense of hopeful expectation within the group, though it may also result in disappointment if the anticipated change does not materialize.

Understanding these basic assumptions allows leaders to recognize the underlying dynamics influencing group behavior. By identifying which assumption a group is operating under, leaders can tailor their approach to meet the group's needs more effectively. For instance, in a group dominated by the dependency assumption, a leader might work to foster greater autonomy and self-reliance among members. Conversely, in a fight-flight scenario, a leader might focus on building cohesion and addressing the perceived threats in a constructive manner. With a group inclined towards the pairing assumption, encouraging collaboration and facilitating the realization of creative potential within the team could be beneficial.

Bion's Basic Assumption Theory illuminates the often-unconscious motivations driving group behavior, providing leaders with a framework to better understand and influence their teams. By acknowledging and addressing these underlying assumptions, leaders can guide their groups towards more adaptive, rational modes of operation, enhancing group cohesion, productivity, and overall effectiveness.

Wilfred Bion introduced the concept of the 'work group' as a counterbalance to the basic assumptions of dependency, fight-flight, and pairing that dominate group dynamics. The work group represents the rational and conscious aspect of group functioning, where members are primarily focused on achieving specific, task-oriented goals. This concept is pivotal in understanding how groups can operate effectively, guided by shared objectives, cooperation, and the practical application of skills and knowledge to accomplish tasks.

The work group is characterized by its commitment to reality and the ability to work through differences and challenges logically and constructively. Unlike the basic assumption modes, which are driven by unconscious needs and can often hinder a group's effectiveness, the work group mode is grounded in mutual understanding, clear communication, and a shared purpose. In this setting, group members engage with one another based on their individual competencies, contributions, and the tasks at hand, rather than unconscious projections or fears.

The role of the work group in achieving task-oriented goals is multifaceted:

1. Rational Decision-Making: The work group encourages a logical and analytical approach to problem-solving, where decisions are made based on evidence, reasoned argument, and the collective expertise of the group members.

2. Effective Communication: Clear and purposeful communication is a hallmark of the work group. This ensures that all members are informed, understand their roles and responsibilities, and are aligned with the group's objectives.

3. Collaboration and Cooperation: The work group fosters an environment where collaboration is valued over competition.

Members are encouraged to contribute their unique skills and knowledge, leading to synergistic outcomes that might not be achievable individually.

4. Adaptability and Learning: Task-oriented groups are open to learning and adaptation. They view challenges and setbacks as opportunities for growth, leading to continuous improvement in processes and outcomes.

5. Leadership and Guidance: In the work group, leadership is often more flexible and dynamic. Leaders facilitate the group's focus on tasks, helping to mediate conflicts, provide direction, and ensure that the group remains goal-oriented. Leadership may also be situational, with different members taking the lead based on their expertise related to specific tasks.

The transition from basic assumption modes to a work group orientation requires awareness and intentional effort from both leaders and group members. Leaders play a crucial role in this transition by recognizing when a group is operating under a basic assumption and using strategies to refocus the group's energy towards task-oriented goals. This may involve setting clear objectives, fostering an environment of trust and respect, encouraging open dialogue about the group's dynamics, and emphasizing the importance of contribution from all members.

The work group is essential for the productive and efficient achievement of goals within organizations. By understanding and cultivating the principles of the work group, leaders can enhance their team's effectiveness, ensuring that unconscious dynamics do not detract from the group's task-oriented objectives. The work group thus serves as a vital counterbalance to the basic assumptions, enabling groups to navigate the complexities of collaboration and achieve success in their collective endeavors.

**The Emotional Experiences of Groups**

Wilfred Bion's insights into the emotional experiences of groups delve into the complex interplay between individual and collective psyches, highlighting how groups can act as containers for individual anxieties. Bion proposed that one of the fundamental functions of a group is to manage the emotional states of its members, particularly their anxieties and fears. This concept is crucial for understanding not only how groups navigate challenges and maintain cohesion but also the role of leadership in facilitating these processes.

Bion observed that groups tend to absorb and mitigate the anxieties of individual members, distributing these emotions across the collective. This diffusion of anxiety serves to lessen the intensity of fear or stress for any one individual, making it more manageable for the group as a whole. However, this dynamic also means that groups can become repositories of shared anxieties, which, if not adequately addressed, can influence group behavior in unconscious and potentially counterproductive ways.

The capacity of a group to act as a container for anxiety is closely related to its ability to maintain a balance between the basic assumption modes and the work group orientation. In the work group mode, where the focus is on task achievement and rational problem-solving, the group is better equipped to manage anxieties constructively. Here, leadership plays a pivotal role in recognizing the signs of emerging anxieties, understanding their potential impact on group dynamics, and employing strategies to address and alleviate these emotions.

Effective leaders facilitate open communication about fears and concerns, creating an environment where emotions can be expressed and explored without judgment. This openness helps to prevent the buildup of unacknowledged anxieties that can disrupt group functioning. Moreover, by acknowledging the group's emotional undercurrents, leaders can guide the group in channeling these emotions into constructive action towards the group's goals.

Leaders also model emotional regulation, demonstrating how to manage anxieties in ways that are conducive to group cohesion and task achievement. This modeling can help to normalize the expression of emotions within the group, encouraging members to view their anxieties as shared challenges that can be overcome through collective effort. His concept of the group as a container for anxiety underscores the importance of developing a group culture that is resilient in the face of stress and change. Groups that have established strong bonds of trust and mutual support are better able to function as effective containers for individual anxieties. These groups are characterized by a sense of solidarity and a collective commitment to navigating challenges together.

Bion's exploration of the emotional experiences of groups provides valuable insights into how groups manage the anxieties of individual members. By acting as containers for these emotions, groups can mitigate the impact of anxiety on individual members and harness their collective strength to maintain focus and effectiveness. Leaders play a crucial role in this process by fostering open communication, modeling emotional regulation, and cultivating a supportive group culture. Through these efforts, leaders can ensure that their groups not only manage anxieties effectively but also thrive in pursuit of their shared objectives.

The impact of group emotions on leadership styles and decision-making processes within teams and organizations is profound and multifaceted. Emotions, both individual and collective, play a crucial role in shaping how leaders lead and how decisions are made and implemented. Understanding the emotional undercurrents within a group can provide leaders with insights into the most effective ways to guide their teams and influence the overall organizational climate.

Influence on Leadership Styles

- Adaptive Leadership: Leaders who are attuned to the emotional experiences of their groups are more likely to adopt an adaptive leadership style. Recognizing the emotional state of the group allows leaders to adjust their approach, whether it means offering more support during times of high stress or challenging the team to grow during periods of complacency. This flexibility is crucial for meeting the group's needs effectively and fostering a positive and productive work environment.

- Transformational Leadership: Group emotions can also influence leaders to adopt a transformational leadership style, where the focus is on inspiring and motivating team members. Leaders who can tap into the group's emotional energy and direct it towards a shared vision or goal can catalyze profound changes in team dynamics and performance. This approach relies on the leader's ability to elevate group emotions, transforming anxiety or uncertainty into enthusiasm and commitment.

- Participative Leadership: When group emotions indicate a need for inclusivity and a sense of belonging, leaders may lean towards a participative style. By involving team members in decision-making processes and valuing their input, leaders can address feelings of disconnection or undervaluation. This style not only improves team morale but also enhances decision-making by incorporating diverse perspectives.

Impact on Decision-Making Processes

- Emotionally Informed Decisions: Leaders who understand the emotional context of their teams are better equipped to make decisions that account for both the rational and emotional needs of the group. This dual consideration can lead to choices that are more broadly supported and more effective in the long term, as they resonate with the team's emotional as well as practical realities.

- Conflict Resolution: Group emotions significantly impact how conflicts are managed and resolved within teams. Leaders who can navigate the emotional landscape of their teams can make decisions that address the root causes of conflicts, rather than merely their symptoms. This approach often involves mediating between differing emotional perspectives to find a resolution that is acceptable to all parties.

- Risk Assessment and Innovation: The collective emotional state of a group can influence its appetite for risk and innovation. Leaders attuned to these emotions can tailor their decision-making to either harness the group's enthusiasm for innovative projects or temper its anxieties about change. This sensitivity ensures that initiatives are launched with a clear understanding of the group's readiness and resilience.

The impact of group emotions on leadership and decision-making is significant, requiring leaders to be emotionally intelligent and responsive. By acknowledging and addressing the emotional dynamics of their teams, leaders can foster environments where positive emotions flourish, enhancing team cohesion, motivation, and overall effectiveness. This emotional attunement also supports more nuanced and considerate decision-making processes, ultimately contributing to the success and well-being of the organization as a whole.

Wilfred Bion's theories, particularly his insights into group dynamics and the emotional experiences of groups, offer a profound lens for understanding the underlying emotional currents that significantly affect team cohesion and organizational culture. By examining groups through Bion's theoretical framework, leaders and organizational development practitioners can gain insights into the often-invisible forces that influence group behavior, decision-making processes, and overall organizational health.

Understanding Team Cohesion

Bion's concept of basic assumptions (dependency, fight-flight, and pairing) highlights the unconscious expectations and behaviors that can emerge within teams, often in response to anxiety or stress. These basic assumptions can undermine team cohesion when unaddressed, as they may lead to dependency on a leader, conflict, or unrealistic expectations of salvation from outside the group. Recognizing these dynamics allows leaders to intervene in ways that move the group towards the 'work group' mentality, where the focus is on rational, task-oriented goals. By addressing the underlying emotional needs and redirecting the group's energy towards shared objectives, leaders can strengthen team cohesion and improve productivity.

## Influencing Organizational Culture

Bion's theories also shed light on the broader emotional currents that shape organizational culture. The collective mood of an organization can often be traced back to the dominant basic assumption modes that pervade its teams and departments. For example, an organizational culture characterized by high levels of anxiety and conflict may be indicative of widespread fight-flight dynamics, while a culture of passivity and reliance on top-down directives may suggest a prevailing dependency mode.

Leaders can use his insights to consciously cultivate an organizational culture that balances emotional well-being with task achievement. This involves creating environments where open communication about emotions and anxieties is encouraged, and where there is a clear commitment to addressing and resolving the underlying issues that fuel unproductive group dynamics. By fostering a culture that values both the emotional and rational contributions of its members, organizations can enhance resilience, adaptability, and a sense of shared purpose.

## Facilitating Change and Development

Bion's work also provides valuable guidance for facilitating change within teams and organizations. Understanding the emotional resistances that can emerge in response to proposed changes—often manifesting in basic assumption behaviors—enables leaders to plan change initiatives that are sensitive to these emotional undercurrents. Leaders can implement strategies that acknowledge and address the fears and anxieties associated with change, thereby reducing resistance and fostering a more supportive atmosphere for transformation.

## Enhancing Leadership Effectiveness

Bion's theories underscore the importance of emotionally intelligent leadership. Leaders who are aware of and can navigate the complex emotional landscapes of their teams can better support their members through challenges, lead more cohesive and motivated teams, and contribute to a positive organizational culture. This involves not just managing the group's task-related activities but also attending to its emotional needs, facilitating a healthy balance between achieving objectives and maintaining emotional well-being. His theories offer a powerful framework for understanding and improving team cohesion and organizational culture. By applying these insights, leaders and organizations can better navigate the emotional dynamics at play, leading to healthier, more productive, and more fulfilling work environments.

## Application to Team and Organizational Dynamics

Wilfred Bion's theories on group dynamics and the emotional experiences of groups provide a nuanced understanding of the subtle, often unconscious, forces that influence team cohesion and organizational culture. These insights are invaluable for leaders and organizational development practitioners aiming to decode and influence the emotional undercurrents within their teams and the wider organization. His identification of basic assumptions—dependency, fight-flight, and pairing—reveals the unconscious expectations and behaviors that emerge within teams, especially under stress or anxiety. Such dynamics can challenge team cohesion, leading to over-dependence on leaders, internal conflicts, or unrealistic expectations for solutions from external sources. Recognizing and addressing these dynamics can guide teams back towards a work-oriented focus, where rational, task-based goals are prioritized, thereby enhancing productivity and strengthening team bonds.

At the organizational level, his framework helps to uncover the emotional currents that define the culture of an organization. Cultures marked by conflict or passivity may reflect widespread underlying assumptions that pervade its teams. Leaders equipped with Bion's insights can strive to nurture an organizational culture that harmonizes emotional well-being with the pursuit of objectives. This is achieved by fostering open dialogues around emotions and anxieties and addressing the root causes of unproductive dynamics, thus building a resilient and adaptive organizational culture. His theories also offer guidance on managing change. Understanding the emotional resistance that can arise, manifesting through basic assumption behaviors, allows leaders to design and implement change initiatives that consider these emotional reactions. By acknowledging and working through these fears and anxieties, organizations can minimize resistance and create a supportive atmosphere for change.

Bion's work highlights the critical role of emotionally intelligent leadership. Leaders who can adeptly navigate their teams' emotional landscapes are better positioned to support their members through challenges, cultivate motivated and cohesive teams, and positively influence organizational culture. This involves a dual focus on managing task-related activities and addressing the group's emotional needs, ensuring a balance between achieving goals and maintaining emotional health. His theoretical contributions offer profound insights for enhancing team cohesion and organizational culture. Applying these insights allows leaders and organizations to navigate emotional dynamics more effectively, fostering work environments that are not only productive but also supportive and fulfilling for all members.

The role of the leader in navigating and managing the dynamics outlined by Wilfred Bion's theories is pivotal in promoting a healthy work environment. Leaders are tasked with the complex challenge of balancing task achievement with emotional well-being, requiring a deep understanding of group dynamics and emotional intelligence. By effectively managing these dynamics, leaders can foster a culture of trust, collaboration, and resilience.

Firstly, leaders must develop an acute awareness of the group's emotional undercurrents and the basic assumption modes in play. This awareness enables them to recognize when a group is operating under the influence of dependency, fight-flight, or pairing dynamics, which can detract from the group's ability to function effectively. By identifying these modes early, leaders can intervene to steer the group back towards a work group orientation, where rational thinking and task-oriented goals prevail.

Leaders play a crucial role in creating an environment where open communication about emotions and anxieties is not just allowed but encouraged. This involves establishing a culture of psychological safety, where team members feel secure in expressing their thoughts and feelings without fear of judgment or repercussion. Such an environment is essential for addressing and resolving the emotional issues that can undermine team cohesion and productivity.

In navigating group dynamics, leaders must also act as emotional regulators for the group. This means being able to maintain calm and steadiness in the face of the group's anxieties and fears. Leaders should model constructive ways to deal with stress and uncertainty, demonstrating emotional resilience and providing a stabilizing influence for their teams. This modeling helps to mitigate the intensity of collective anxieties and guides the team towards more adaptive responses to challenges. Additionally, leaders should actively work to promote team cohesion by emphasizing shared goals and values. This involves not only aligning the team around a common purpose but also recognizing and valuing the unique contributions of each team member. By fostering a sense of belonging and significance within the team, leaders can combat feelings of isolation and encourage a more collaborative and supportive team dynamic.

Leaders must also be adept at facilitating change and development within their teams. This includes being sensitive to the emotional responses that change can evoke and employing strategies to manage these responses constructively. Whether through providing reassurance, clarifying the rationale for change, or involving team members in the change process, leaders can help to ease the transition and maintain a focus on the group's objectives.

A leader's commitment to their own personal and professional development is key to successfully managing group dynamics. By continuously seeking to enhance their understanding of group behavior and emotional intelligence, leaders can improve their ability to navigate complex emotional landscapes. This ongoing development ensures that leaders remain effective in their role, capable of adapting their leadership style to meet the evolving needs of their team and organization. The leader's role in navigating and managing group dynamics, as described by Bion's theories, is central to promoting a healthy work environment. Through awareness, communication, emotional regulation, and a commitment to team cohesion and personal growth, leaders can ensure that their teams are not only productive but also emotionally resilient and engaged.

**Managing Team Anxiety**

Leaders can employ several strategies to manage team anxiety effectively, drawing on Bion's concepts of containment and the work group. These strategies help in navigating the emotional undercurrents within teams and fostering a supportive and productive work environment:

1. Create a Safe Space for Expression: Encourage open dialogue where team members can express their concerns and anxieties without fear of judgment. This creates a sense of psychological safety, essential for addressing and working through collective anxieties.

2. Model Emotional Regulation: Demonstrate how to manage anxieties constructively by staying calm and composed in stressful situations. Leaders who regulate their emotions effectively can serve as a stabilizing force within the team, reducing collective anxiety.

3. Normalize the Discussion of Anxiety: Make it clear that experiencing anxiety, especially during periods of change or uncertainty, is normal. By normalizing these feelings, leaders

can prevent the stigma associated with anxiety, making it easier for team members to share and address their concerns.

4. Focus on the Work Group Orientation: Guide the team towards a task-oriented focus, where the emphasis is on achieving specific goals. This helps in redirecting the team's energy away from unproductive anxieties towards constructive activities.

5. Provide Clarity and Direction: Often, anxiety stems from uncertainty about roles, expectations, or the future. Leaders can alleviate these anxieties by providing clear direction, defining roles and responsibilities, and communicating openly about future plans and changes.

6. Use Containment to Manage Emotions: Act as a container for the team's anxieties by acknowledging and validating these emotions without becoming overwhelmed by them. This involves actively listening to concerns, offering reassurance, and working with the team to find solutions.

7. Encourage Problem-Solving: Involve the team in identifying the root causes of their anxiety and brainstorming solutions. This empowers team members and can transform anxiety into action.

8. Build Resilience: Foster team resilience by highlighting past successes and how the team has overcome previous challenges. This builds confidence in the team's ability to handle future anxieties and stresses.

9. Offer Support and Resources: Ensure that team members have access to resources and support, whether through formal programs, training in stress management techniques, or informal peer support systems.

By integrating these strategies, leaders can manage team anxiety more effectively, ensuring that their teams remain cohesive, focused, and productive even in the face of challenges.

Leaders play a crucial role in identifying and constructively addressing signs of anxiety within their teams, ensuring the maintenance of a healthy, productive work environment. Recognizing anxiety's manifestations is the first step, which can include noticeable changes in team members' behavior, such as irritability or withdrawal, a decline in productivity, increased absenteeism, breakdowns in communication, and even physical symptoms like fatigue or changes in appetite.

Once these signs are identified, leaders should adopt a multifaceted approach to address the underlying issues. Creating an environment that encourages open dialogue is essential. By regularly checking in with team members and maintaining an open-door policy, leaders can foster a culture where concerns and anxieties can be shared freely. Validating team members' feelings by acknowledging their stress and anxiety can significantly alleviate their sense of isolation, making them feel understood and supported.

Clarity and reassurance are powerful tools against anxiety, particularly when it stems from uncertainty. Leaders should communicate clearly about any changes, expectations, and future plans, providing the reassurance needed to mitigate fears about job security or performance expectations. Where possible, offering flexibility in work arrangements can also help team members manage their workload and reduce stress levels. Promoting a supportive team culture is another critical aspect, where team members are encouraged to support each other, thereby strengthening team bonds and reducing feelings of isolation. Leaders should also provide resources and training on managing stress and building resilience, equipping team members with the tools they need to handle anxiety more effectively.

Leading by example, by demonstrating a healthy work-life balance and stress management practices, can inspire team members to adopt similar habits. For those needing more specialized support, leaders should encourage the use of professional mental health resources, such as employee assistance programs.

In addressing team anxiety, the goal is not just to maintain productivity but to nurture a supportive, empathetic work environment. This approach ensures that team members feel valued and heard, contributing to the overall health and success of the organization.

## Fostering Effective Group Functioning

The application of Wilfred Bion's theories to fostering effective group functioning presents a nuanced approach to leadership that emphasizes the balance between task-oriented goals and the emotional needs of the group. Bion's insights into group dynamics, particularly his distinction between the work group and basic assumption groups, provide a framework for understanding how leaders can guide their teams towards productivity while addressing the underlying emotional currents that influence group behavior.

At the core of Bion's theory is the concept that for a group to function effectively, it must navigate between focusing on the task at hand (the work group) and managing the emotional and unconscious processes (basic assumption modes) that can derail its efforts. The work group is characterized by its commitment to achieving specific, rational objectives through cooperation and the practical application of skills. In contrast, basic assumption modes—dependency, fight-flight, and pairing—are driven by the group's unconscious needs and can lead to behaviors that undermine its task-oriented focus.

Balancing Task-Oriented Goals

To foster effective group functioning, leaders must first ensure that the group's task-oriented goals are clear, achievable, and understood by all members. This involves setting specific objectives, defining roles and responsibilities, and establishing metrics for success. By maintaining a strong focus on the work group orientation, leaders can guide the group's energy towards productive endeavors.

## Addressing Emotional Needs

Equally important is the leader's role in addressing the emotional needs of the group. This requires leaders to be attuned to the group's emotional undercurrents and to recognize when basic assumption modes are influencing behavior. For example, in a group operating under the dependency assumption, members may look to the leader for direction and reassurance. Leaders can address this by fostering autonomy within the group, encouraging decision-making and problem-solving at the individual and collective levels.

In groups dominated by fight-flight dynamics, where conflict or avoidance behaviors emerge, leaders must work to build cohesion and address the underlying fears or tensions driving these behaviors. This may involve conflict resolution strategies, team-building activities, or open discussions about the group's concerns and how they can be collectively addressed.

## Facilitating the Transition to Work Group Orientation

Leaders play a critical role in facilitating the group's transition from basic assumption modes to a work group orientation. This involves creating an environment where emotional expressions are acknowledged and managed constructively. Leaders can model this behavior by demonstrating emotional regulation, offering support, and encouraging open communication. By validating the group's emotions and providing a containment function, leaders can help the group process its anxieties and refocus on its tasks.

Leaders can enhance group functioning by promoting a culture of reflection and learning. Encouraging the group to reflect on its experiences, both successes and failures, can provide valuable insights into how it can improve its task-oriented focus while also attending to its emotional well-being. The application of Bion's theories to fostering effective group functioning requires a balanced approach that addresses both the task-oriented goals and the emotional needs of the group. By maintaining this balance, leaders can guide their teams towards high performance, resilience, and a positive, supportive work environment.

Facilitating transitions between basic assumption modes and the work group is a critical task for leaders aiming to enhance team productivity and satisfaction. This process requires leaders to be attuned to the emotional undercurrents of their teams and to employ strategies that encourage a focus on task-oriented goals while addressing the group's underlying emotional needs. They can begin by fostering a deep understanding of the group's dynamics. Recognizing when a team is operating under one of Bion's basic assumption modes—dependency, fight-flight, or pairing—is essential. Such modes, while a natural part of group dynamics, can hinder productivity if they become the group's dominant way of functioning. Leaders should look for signs like over-reliance on the leader for direction, avoidance of challenging tasks, or unrealistic expectations for solutions from within the group.

Once a leader identifies the prevailing basic assumption mode, they can take steps to guide the group back towards a work group orientation. This involves reinforcing the purpose and goals of the team, clarifying roles, and setting clear, achievable tasks. Leaders should ensure that all team members understand how their contributions fit into the larger objectives, thereby fostering a sense of purpose and direction.

Addressing the emotional needs of the group is also crucial. Leaders can create an environment where team members feel safe to express their concerns and anxieties. This might involve regular check-ins, creating forums for open discussion, or one-on-one meetings where team members can voice their feelings without fear of judgment. By acknowledging and validating these emotions, leaders can help mitigate the anxieties driving basic assumption behaviors.

Promoting autonomy within the team helps to counter dependency modes. Encouraging decision-making and problem-solving at the individual and team levels empowers members, boosting their confidence and reducing their reliance on the leader for every decision. This shift not only enhances productivity but also team satisfaction, as members feel more engaged and valued for their contributions. In teams dominated by fight-flight dynamics, leaders should focus on building cohesion and trust. This might involve team-building activities, conflict resolution training, or facilitated discussions aimed at addressing underlying tensions. By promoting a culture of mutual respect and collaboration, leaders can help their teams navigate conflicts constructively and focus on common goals. Leaders can also leverage the pairing assumption positively by fostering a culture of mentorship and collaboration. Encouraging team members to work in pairs or small groups on specific tasks or projects can harness the creative and productive potential of this basic assumption mode, leading to innovative solutions and stronger team bonds.

The transition from basic assumption modes to a work group orientation requires leaders to balance task-oriented leadership with emotional intelligence. By actively managing the group's dynamics, addressing emotional needs, and fostering an environment focused on achievement and collaboration, leaders can enhance both team productivity and satisfaction. This balanced approach ensures that teams are not only effective in their tasks but also resilient, adaptable, and cohesive in the face of challenges.

### Bion's Relevance to Modern Leadership Challenges

Wilfred Bion's theories on group dynamics and emotional experiences provide insightful frameworks for addressing contemporary leadership challenges. His concepts of basic assumption modes, the work group, and the importance of containing anxiety are particularly relevant to modern issues like remote team management, organizational change, and diversity and inclusion. These challenges, while distinct, share a common need for leaders to navigate complex emotional landscapes and foster cohesive, adaptive teams.

Remote Team Management

The shift towards remote work has underscored the importance of understanding and managing the emotional undercurrents within teams. Bion's concept of containment is crucial here, as remote teams may experience heightened feelings of isolation, anxiety, and dependency on leadership for guidance and reassurance. Leaders can apply Bion's theories by creating virtual spaces for open communication, encouraging team members to share their concerns and anxieties. By acknowledging and addressing these emotions, leaders can mitigate feelings of disconnection and promote a sense of belonging and cohesion, even in a virtual environment.

Organizational Change

Organizational change often triggers uncertainty and anxiety, leading teams to revert to basic assumption modes as they grapple with the unknown. Leaders managing change can draw on Bion's work to recognize and address these emotional responses constructively. For example, a team might exhibit fight-flight behavior, resisting change due to perceived threats to their status or security. Leaders can use containment strategies to acknowledge these fears, provide reassurance, and refocus the team on the work group orientation by clearly articulating the vision and benefits of the change, thereby facilitating a smoother transition.

Diversity and Inclusion

Diversity and inclusion efforts can also benefit from Bion's insights into group dynamics. These initiatives often challenge existing norms and may surface unconscious biases and anxieties within teams. Leaders can apply Bion's concepts to create an environment where all team members feel valued and understood, addressing the dependency needs for security and belonging. By fostering open dialogue about diversity and inclusion, leaders can help their teams move beyond fight-flight or pairing responses, encouraging a focus on shared goals and the benefits of a diverse, inclusive work culture. This approach not only enhances team cohesion but also leverages diverse perspectives for greater creativity and innovation.

In each of these contexts, Bion's theories offer leaders tools for understanding and navigating the emotional dynamics that influence team behavior and cohesion. By applying these insights, leaders can enhance their teams' resilience, adaptability, and effectiveness, ensuring that they are equipped to meet the challenges of the modern workplace. Whether managing remote teams, guiding organizational change, or advancing diversity and inclusion, leaders can draw on Bion's work to foster environments where emotional well-being and task-oriented focus are balanced, leading to healthier, more productive organizational cultures.

The ongoing relevance of understanding group dynamics becomes increasingly critical in today's complex and interconnected work environment. As organizations navigate rapid technological advances, globalization, and shifting societal expectations, the ability to manage and lead diverse teams effectively has never been more important. Wilfred Bion's exploration of group dynamics offers invaluable insights for leaders striving to create cohesive, adaptive, and high-performing teams amidst these challenges.

In an era where remote work and digital collaboration have become commonplace, the nuances of group dynamics play a pivotal role in ensuring team cohesion and productivity. The virtual work environment can amplify feelings of isolation and disconnect, making Bion's concepts of containment and the work group essential for leaders to foster a sense of belonging and collective focus. By understanding the emotional needs of their teams and creating spaces for open dialogue, leaders can mitigate the negative impacts of physical distance on team dynamics. Furthermore, the pace and scale of organizational change have accelerated, making it imperative for leaders to manage the anxieties and resistances such changes often provoke. Bion's insights into how groups react under stress—gravitating towards basic assumption modes—can help leaders anticipate and address these emotional responses. By applying strategies that balance emotional containment with a clear focus on task-oriented goals, leaders can guide their teams through transitions more effectively, minimizing disruption and maintaining morale.

The increasing emphasis on diversity and inclusion in the workplace also underscores the importance of understanding group dynamics. Diverse teams bring a range of perspectives and experiences that can enrich decision-making and spur innovation. However, navigating the complexities of diverse group identities requires leaders to be adept at managing the varied emotional responses and potential conflicts that can arise. Bion's framework provides a lens through which leaders can recognize and address these dynamics, ensuring that all team members feel valued and included, thereby enhancing team performance and cohesion.

The interconnectedness of the modern work environment means that decisions and actions within one team or department can have wide-reaching effects across the organization and beyond. Leaders must therefore be capable of not just managing the dynamics within their own teams but also understanding how these dynamics interact with and impact the broader organizational culture and stakeholder relationships. This interconnectedness demands a deep understanding of group behavior and the emotional undercurrents that influence it.

The complexities of today's work environment make the understanding of group dynamics not just relevant but essential for effective leadership. The insights provided by Bion and other theorists in this field equip leaders with the knowledge and skills to navigate the emotional landscapes of their teams, fostering environments that support both individual well-being and organizational objectives. As work continues to evolve, the principles of group dynamics will remain a cornerstone for building resilient, innovative, and cohesive teams capable of thriving in an increasingly complex world.

**Case Studies**

The hypothetical case studies illustrate the power of Bion's concepts in addressing contemporary leadership and organizational challenges. By understanding and applying principles of containment and the work group orientation, leaders can navigate their teams through periods of uncertainty and change, fostering environments that support both task achievement and emotional well-being.

Case Study 1: Navigating Remote Team Dynamics

A tech company's transition to fully remote work during a global crisis led to significant stress and anxiety among its development team. The team struggled with feelings of isolation, dependency on leadership for reassurance, and difficulties in maintaining productivity.

The team leader observed increased signs of dependency, with team members frequently seeking guidance for tasks they previously handled independently. Additionally, there was a noticeable decline in creative collaboration, a key component of the team's success.

Recognizing the shift towards a dependency mode, the leader decided to apply Bion's concept of containment. They began by organizing regular virtual check-in meetings designed not just for project updates but as forums for expressing concerns and anxieties. The leader emphasized the importance of these sessions as safe spaces, encouraging openness and vulnerability. To transition the team towards a work group orientation, the leader introduced structured brainstorming sessions to foster creative problem-solving and reduce the dependency dynamic. They highlighted each member's unique contributions and encouraged autonomy by assigning leadership roles in projects based on members' strengths.

Over time, the team began to exhibit more confidence in their abilities to work independently and collaboratively tackle challenges. The emphasis on containment and transitioning to a work group orientation led to a noticeable improvement in productivity and a revitalization of the creative synergy that had defined the team pre-remote work. The team reported feeling more connected and supported, despite the physical distance.

Case Study 2: Leading Through Organizational Change

A multinational corporation was undergoing a significant organizational restructuring that triggered widespread anxiety and resistance among employees. The leadership team noticed an increase in fight-flight behaviors, with departments either openly resisting the changes or withdrawing from participation in the change process.

The CEO needed to address the pervasive anxiety undermining the restructuring process, preventing the organization from moving forward with its strategic goals.

Drawing on Bion's insights, the CEO implemented a series of town hall meetings aimed at containing the group's anxieties. These meetings were designed to acknowledge the emotional turmoil the changes had caused and provide a platform for employees to voice their concerns and fears. Simultaneously, the CEO worked with department heads to cultivate a work group atmosphere, focusing on the tasks at hand and how each department fit into the broader vision for the organization's future. This involved clearly defining roles within the new structure and setting short-term goals to guide departments through the transition. To address the fight-flight dynamics, the CEO and department heads engaged in transparent communication about the reasons for the change, the benefits to the organization and its employees, and the support available to help employees adapt.

The containment strategies, coupled with a clear focus on task-oriented goals and transparent communication, gradually eased the organization's transition. Employees began to engage more constructively with the change process, moving from resistance to active participation. The organization successfully navigated the restructuring, emerging more cohesive and aligned with its strategic vision.

# Conclusion

The exploration of Wilfred Bion's work on group dynamics culminates in a profound understanding of the intricate balance between task-oriented goals and the emotional needs of teams. Bion's insights into the basic assumption modes and the work group offer leaders a powerful lens through which to view and influence group behavior, emphasizing the critical role of emotional undercurrents in team cohesion and productivity.

Key insights from Bion's work highlight that groups often oscillate between task-oriented activities and underlying emotional processes that can either enhance or hinder their ability to achieve objectives. The basic assumption modes—dependency, fight-flight, and pairing—serve as mechanisms through which groups manage anxiety and uncertainty, yet they can lead teams away from their core tasks if not properly managed. The work group concept, on the other hand, represents the group's capacity to engage in rational, objective-focused work, providing a counterbalance to the potentially disruptive effects of basic assumption modes.

For leaders, the application of Bion's theories underscores the importance of being attuned to the emotional states of their teams. Recognizing when a team is operating under a basic assumption mode allows leaders to intervene in ways that gently steer the group back towards a work group orientation. This might involve creating spaces for open dialogue, where team members can express anxieties and concerns, thereby reducing the hold of unconscious processes on the group's behavior. His concept of containment is particularly relevant for leaders aiming to foster a supportive and productive work environment. By acting as containers for their teams' anxieties, leaders can help to mitigate the impact of stress and uncertainty, enabling team members to focus on their tasks with greater clarity and commitment. This process requires leaders to demonstrate emotional intelligence, sensitivity, and the ability to regulate their own responses to effectively manage the group's emotional dynamics.

The implications of Bion's work for leadership and organizational behavior are far-reaching. In today's complex and often rapidly changing work environment, the ability to navigate both the rational and emotional aspects of group functioning is indispensable. Leaders who can balance these dimensions are better equipped to guide their teams through challenges, foster innovation, and achieve sustained organizational success. His theories on group dynamics enrich our understanding of leadership in fundamental ways. They remind us that effective leadership is not solely about strategic thinking and decision-making but also about being deeply attuned to the emotional undercurrents of our teams. This attunement is a critical component of effective leadership, essential for building resilient, cohesive, and high-performing teams. As organizations continue to evolve, the insights derived from Bion's work will undoubtedly remain a vital resource for leaders seeking to navigate the complexities of group dynamics in the pursuit of organizational excellence.

In light of the rich insights derived from Wilfred Bion's exploration of group dynamics, leaders are encouraged to apply these concepts as a practical framework within their own organizations. Bion's theories, centered on the basic assumption modes, the work group, and the vital role of containment, offer leaders a robust set of tools for understanding and enhancing the complex dynamics that underpin team and organizational behavior.

Applying Bion's concepts enables leaders to navigate the often-invisible emotional undercurrents that influence group functioning, providing a pathway to more effective, responsive, and empathetic leadership. By recognizing the signs of basic assumption modes at play within teams—whether it's dependency, fight-flight, or pairing—leaders can take proactive steps to address these dynamics, steering groups back towards a productive work group orientation focused on achieving collective goals.

Bion's emphasis on the leader's role in containing and managing group anxieties highlights the importance of emotional intelligence in leadership. Creating a space where team members feel safe to express their concerns and anxieties not only mitigates the disruptive impact of these emotions but also fosters a culture of trust, openness, and mutual support. This, in turn, enhances team cohesion, resilience, and the capacity to tackle challenges collaboratively.

Leaders are encouraged to view Bion's framework not as a prescriptive set of rules but as a flexible guide for enhancing group dynamics. This involves a commitment to ongoing learning and adaptation, as leaders become more attuned to the emotional landscapes of their teams and more skilled in navigating these dynamics effectively. Practical steps such as regular team check-ins, open forums for discussion, and targeted team-building activities can all serve as avenues for applying Bion's concepts in day-to-day leadership practice.

Integrating Bion's insights into leadership development programs can equip emerging leaders with the knowledge and skills necessary to manage group dynamics effectively. This ensures that the organization cultivates a cadre of leaders who are not only strategically competent but also emotionally intelligent and adept at fostering healthy, productive team environments.

Bion's work offers a valuable perspective on leadership that is increasingly relevant in today's complex organizational landscapes. By applying his concepts, leaders can deepen their understanding of group dynamics, enhance their leadership effectiveness, and contribute to building organizations that are not only successful but also supportive and adaptive. Leaders are thus encouraged to explore and integrate Bion's theories into their leadership practices, leveraging these insights to enrich the dynamics within their teams and across their organizations.

# Chapter 5: Kurt Lewin and Leadership Styles

Kurt Lewin, often hailed as the father of modern social psychology, made pioneering contributions that have deeply influenced our understanding of group dynamics, organizational behavior, and the psychology of change. His work laid the groundwork for much of contemporary leadership theory, offering insights that remain crucial for leaders navigating the complexities of today's organizational landscapes.

Lewin's research in the early to mid-20th century introduced several key concepts that have become foundational to the field of leadership studies. Among these, his identification of different leadership styles—autocratic, democratic, and laissez-faire—provided a framework for understanding how leaders' approaches to management can significantly impact group behavior, motivation, and productivity. These styles, characterized by varying degrees of leader control and group participation, have been instrumental in shaping theories of effective leadership and organizational development.

In addition to his work on leadership styles, Lewin developed the force field analysis model, a tool for understanding the factors that influence change within groups and organizations. This model posits that any given state of affairs is maintained by the balance between forces driving change and those resisting it. Lewin's force field analysis has become a vital strategy for leaders and change agents, offering a method for diagnosing problems, planning change initiatives, and managing the resistance that invariably accompanies organizational transformation.

His emphasis on the importance of understanding group dynamics and the psychological underpinnings of resistance to change underscores the role of leadership in facilitating effective change management. His insights into the social processes that govern group behavior and his innovative approaches to studying these processes have had a lasting impact on how leaders approach the challenges of motivating teams, driving change, and fostering organizational resilience.

As we delve into Lewin's leadership styles and the force field analysis model, we explore their enduring relevance and application in addressing modern leadership challenges. These concepts not only provide leaders with a deeper understanding of their own leadership impact but also equip them with practical tools for navigating the dynamics of change and enhancing organizational performance. Lewin's work serves as a testament to the power of integrating psychological insights into leadership practice, offering valuable lessons for leaders seeking to cultivate adaptive, high-performing teams.

## Lewin's Leadership Styles

Kurt Lewin's exploration into leadership styles marked a significant contribution to our understanding of group behavior and organizational psychology. He categorized leadership styles into three distinct types: autocratic, democratic, and laissez-faire, each with its unique psychological underpinnings and behavioral characteristics. These styles illuminate the various ways leaders can influence team dynamics, motivation, and performance.

Autocratic Leadership Style

The autocratic style is characterized by a high degree of leader control over all decision-making processes, with little to no input from team members. Psychologically, this style is underpinned by a belief in the efficiency of centralized decision-making and a low level of trust in the team's ability to contribute to critical decisions. Behaviorally, autocratic leaders tend to issue orders, dictate methods, and expect compliance without question. While this style can lead to quick decision-making and is sometimes effective in crisis situations, it can also suppress creativity, reduce team morale, and lead to higher levels of dependence on the leader.

Lewin's research found that autocratic leadership tends to produce a work environment with high levels of efficiency and productivity in the short term. However, this style also led to increased tension, less creativity, and lower satisfaction among team members. Groups under autocratic leadership showed higher levels of dependency on the leader, with diminished initiative and self-reliance. The lack of involvement in decision-making processes often resulted in passive resistance, reduced morale, and a higher likelihood of aggression or apathy within the group.

Democratic Leadership Style

Democratic leadership, in contrast, is marked by a participative approach to decision-making, where team members are encouraged to contribute ideas and opinions. This style is based on the psychological belief in the value of shared leadership and trust in the team's capacity for self-direction. Democratic leaders facilitate group discussions, encourage collaboration, and support consensus-building processes. The behavioral characteristics of this style include active listening, open communication, and a commitment to fostering team involvement. The democratic approach can enhance team satisfaction, creativity, and ownership of outcomes, though decision-making processes may take longer than in autocratic settings.

Democratic leadership, by contrast, was shown to foster a more engaged and cohesive group dynamic. Teams led by democratic leaders exhibited higher levels of creativity and satisfaction, as members felt valued and empowered to contribute their ideas and perspectives. Lewin's research highlighted that democratic leadership encourages higher levels of participation and collaboration, leading to more sustainable motivation and commitment among team members. Although decision-making processes might take longer due to the emphasis on consensus and participation, the outcomes often enjoyed greater support and commitment from the entire group, enhancing the quality and durability of performance.

## Laissez-faire Leadership Style

Laissez-faire leadership is defined by a hands-off approach, where the leader provides minimal direction and allows team members to manage their own tasks and make decisions independently. The psychological underpinning of this style is a high level of trust in the team's abilities and self-motivation. Behaviorally, laissez-faire leaders step back, offering support and resources as needed but largely delegating authority to team members. While this style can foster innovation and independence, it can also lead to confusion, lack of cohesion, and inconsistent performance if not implemented with clear boundaries and support structures.

Lewin's findings on laissez-faire leadership revealed a mixed impact on group behavior and performance. While this style provided team members with a high degree of autonomy and freedom, it often resulted in lower levels of productivity and coherence within the group. Without clear direction and support from the leader, teams sometimes struggled with organization, prioritization, and decision-making. However, in contexts where team members were highly skilled, self-motivated, and possessed strong self-direction, laissez-faire leadership could lead to innovative solutions and high levels of satisfaction.

Each of Lewin's leadership styles offers different advantages and challenges, and the effectiveness of each style can vary depending on the context, the nature of the task, and the team's composition. Understanding these styles allows leaders to adapt their approach to best meet the needs of their team and the demands of the situation, demonstrating Lewin's lasting impact on the field of leadership and organizational development.

Lewin's research underscores the critical role of leadership style in shaping the psychological climate of a team, which in turn affects motivation, behavior, and performance. The democratic style emerged as particularly effective in promoting a positive group dynamic, fostering creativity, and ensuring sustained motivation and performance over time. However, Lewin also emphasized the importance of context in choosing the most appropriate leadership style, suggesting that leaders need to adapt their approach based on the specific needs of the team and the demands of the situation. Lewin's seminal work on leadership styles offers valuable insights into the complex interplay between leadership approaches and group dynamics. By understanding the impact of different leadership styles, leaders can make more informed choices that enhance team cohesion, motivation, and performance, ultimately contributing to the success of their organizations.

Kurt Lewin's research into leadership styles has had a profound impact on our understanding of how different approaches to leadership can influence group behavior, motivation, and performance. Through his experiments and observations, Lewin and his colleagues were able to draw significant conclusions about the effects of autocratic, democratic, and laissez-faire leadership on teams. These findings have continued to inform leadership practices and organizational development strategies across various contexts.

## Psychological Foundations of Leadership Styles

Kurt Lewin's categorization of leadership styles—autocratic, democratic, and laissez-faire—draws upon deep psychological foundations, particularly in the realms of group dynamics, social influence, and the human need for belonging. These psychological underpinnings offer a rich context for understanding how different leadership styles impact group behavior and performance.

At the heart of Lewin's leadership styles is the concept of group dynamics, which explores the psychological processes that occur when individuals interact within a group. Lewin posited that the behavior of an individual in a group is not just a result of their personal characteristics but is also profoundly influenced by the group's collective dynamics. This perspective highlights the role of leadership in shaping these dynamics, where different styles can either facilitate or hinder the development of positive group interactions and cohesion.

Social influence theory also plays a crucial role in Lewin's leadership styles. This theory examines how individuals' attitudes, beliefs, and behaviors are shaped by those around them. In the context of leadership, this means that a leader's behavior and approach to managing the group can significantly influence team members' motivation, satisfaction, and performance. For instance, democratic leadership fosters an environment of mutual respect and collaboration, encouraging team members to actively participate and invest in the group's objectives. In contrast, autocratic leadership may stifle individual expression and initiative, leading to compliance out of obligation rather than genuine commitment.

The need for belonging is another critical psychological concept that informs Lewin's leadership styles. Humans have an innate desire to be part of a community and to feel connected to others. Leadership styles can affect how well this need is met within a group. Democratic leadership, by valuing each member's input and fostering a sense of inclusivity, can satisfy this need, enhancing team cohesion and loyalty. Laissez-faire leadership, while offering freedom, may neglect this need if there is insufficient support and guidance, potentially leading to feelings of isolation among team members. Autocratic leadership might provide a clear structure and sense of belonging through shared goals, but it may also limit individual autonomy and expression, affecting team members' sense of personal investment in the group.

Lewin's leadership styles are grounded in these psychological theories, illustrating the complex interplay between a leader's approach and the psychological needs and dynamics of their team. Understanding these foundations can help leaders choose the most appropriate style to foster a productive, cohesive, and motivated team environment, tailored to the unique needs and circumstances of their group. By applying these insights, leaders can navigate the challenges of group management more effectively, creating environments where individuals feel valued, connected, and committed to their collective goals.

A leader's psychological orientation and personal history play a significant role in shaping their preferred leadership style. The interplay of an individual's personality traits, past experiences, values, and beliefs can significantly influence how they approach leadership, impacting everything from decision-making processes to how they interact with team members.

Leaders with a history of positive, collaborative experiences may gravitate towards a democratic leadership style. Their past successes with teamwork and shared decision-making likely reinforce the belief in the value of collective input and consensus. This orientation emphasizes trust in the team's capabilities and a genuine desire to foster an inclusive and participative work environment. Such leaders often believe in the empowerment of team members, encouraging autonomy and personal growth within the framework of achieving common goals.

Conversely, leaders who have experienced efficiency and quick decision-making in high-stress or crisis situations may develop a preference for an autocratic leadership style. Their psychological orientation might be influenced by a need for control and a belief in the effectiveness of centralized decision-making. This could stem from past environments where rapid, decisive action was rewarded or where the consequences of failure were particularly high. Such leaders might prioritize outcomes and efficiency over process, believing that this approach is the best way to achieve organizational objectives.

Individuals with a laissez-faire orientation towards leadership often possess a high level of trust in their team's abilities and motivation. This trust might be rooted in their personal history of working independently or in environments where autonomy and self-direction were highly valued. Leaders with this orientation might believe strongly in the principle that people perform best when they are given the freedom to utilize their skills and creativity without micromanagement. Their leadership style reflects a hands-off approach, providing support and resources as needed but otherwise allowing team members to navigate their own paths to task completion.

The psychological orientation of a leader also influences how they handle conflict, stress, and uncertainty. Leaders who have developed resilience and adaptability through their life experiences might be more inclined to adopt a democratic or laissez-faire style, comfortable with navigating the complexities of group dynamics and change. In contrast, leaders whose experiences have conditioned them to view control as a means to mitigate risk might prefer an autocratic style, especially in situations perceived as volatile or high stakes.

A leader's psychological orientation and personal history are critical determinants of their leadership style. These factors shape their perceptions of effectiveness, their interactions with team members, and their strategies for achieving organizational goals. By reflecting on their own orientations and histories, leaders can gain valuable insights into their leadership behaviors, potentially identifying areas for growth and adaptation to meet the needs of their teams and organizations more effectively.

**Force Field Analysis Model**

Kurt Lewin's force field analysis model is a pivotal concept in understanding the dynamics of organizational change. This model provides a framework for diagnosing situations, identifying factors that promote or hinder progress toward a desired state, and developing strategies for managing change effectively. At its core, the force field analysis is predicated on the idea that any situation is the result of competing forces: those seeking to promote change (driving forces) and those attempting to maintain the status quo (restraining forces).

Driving Forces

Driving forces are those factors within an organization that push towards a change. These can include internal pressures such as the recognition of a need for improved efficiency or performance, technological advancements, shifts in employee attitudes, or external pressures like market competition, regulatory changes, and evolving customer needs. Driving forces motivate the organization to move away from its current state towards a new, improved state. They are essentially the source of energy and momentum for change.

Restraining Forces

In contrast, restraining forces are elements that resist the push for change. These can stem from a variety of sources, such as organizational inertia, existing processes and systems that are incompatible with the new direction, cultural norms and values that favor the status quo, employee fears and uncertainties regarding the change, and potential losses for those who benefit from existing conditions. Restraining forces act as barriers to change, slowing down or completely halting the progress toward the desired state.

Lewin's model emphasizes that for change to occur, the balance between these competing forces must be altered. This can be achieved by either strengthening the driving forces, weakening the restraining forces, or a combination of both. Force field analysis involves a step-by-step process:

1. Identifying the desired state or goal of the change initiative.

2. Listing all the driving forces that support the change.

3. Listing all the restraining forces that oppose the change.

4. Assessing the strength and influence of each force.

5. Developing strategies to strengthen driving forces or weaken restraining forces.

The force field analysis model is particularly useful in strategic planning and decision-making processes. It helps leaders and change agents to visualize the complexities of change, anticipate resistance, and plan interventions that address the specific conditions of their organizational context. By understanding and actively managing the forces at play, organizations can increase the likelihood of successful change implementation, ensuring that transitions are smoother and more sustainable.

Lewin's force field analysis offers a pragmatic approach to change management, providing leaders with the tools to navigate the multifaceted challenges of guiding their organizations through transformation. It underscores the importance of a balanced assessment of both the motivators and obstacles to change, facilitating a more informed and strategic approach to achieving organizational objectives.

Leaders can harness Kurt Lewin's force field analysis as a strategic tool for planning and executing change initiatives by taking a nuanced look at the psychological and situational factors that influence organizational dynamics. The process begins with a clear articulation of the desired change, ensuring that the vision and objectives are compelling and understood across the organization. This clarity is foundational for identifying the forces that will drive the change forward and those that will resist it. Engaging with stakeholders at all levels through open communication channels like surveys, interviews, and discussions is critical for mapping out these forces comprehensively.

Evaluating the strength and impact of each identified force allows leaders to prioritize their efforts effectively, concentrating on the most influential factors. To amplify driving forces, strategies might include enhancing communication to articulate the benefits of the change clearly, engaging employees in the change process to cultivate buy-in and modifying organizational structures and processes to align with the new direction. Simultaneously, addressing restraining forces is essential for mitigating resistance. Leaders can tackle employees' fears and concerns by offering reassurance, providing necessary training, and ensuring access to resources that facilitate adaptation to change. Recognizing and validating these concerns plays a significant role in reducing opposition to the change.

As the change is implemented, continuous monitoring is vital to gauge the initiative's progress and the ongoing interplay of driving and restraining forces. This vigilance allows for real-time adjustments, ensuring the initiative remains aligned with its objectives. Moreover, fostering an organizational culture that prizes flexibility, continuous learning, and adaptability prepares the ground for a resilient and dynamic organization, more adept at navigating future changes.

By applying force field analysis in this comprehensive and strategic manner, leaders can approach change initiatives with a deep understanding of the complex dynamics at play. Considering both the psychological motivations and situational realities within the organization leads to more effective change strategies. This holistic approach not only supports the successful implementation of change initiatives but also promotes a healthier organizational environment, capable of thriving amidst the challenges and opportunities of the contemporary business world.

**Application to Organizational Change**

Applying Kurt Lewin's leadership styles and force field analysis to manage organizational change involves a nuanced understanding of the dynamics between leadership, employee engagement, and resistance. Leaders can navigate these complexities by adopting a strategic approach that aligns with Lewin's principles, ensuring that change initiatives are not only implemented successfully but also sustainably embraced by the organization.

At the outset, leaders should assess their predominant leadership style and adapt it to the needs of the change initiative. For instance, while an autocratic style might be effective in the initial stages of a change for quick decision-making, transitioning to a more democratic style can foster employee engagement and participation as the change progresses. This shift encourages a sense of ownership among team members, making them more likely to support the change.

Lewin's force field analysis offers a framework for identifying the driving and restraining forces related to the change. Leaders can use this analysis to develop a comprehensive strategy that strengthens driving forces—such as the vision for change, incentives for employees, and the support of key stakeholders—while addressing and minimizing restraining forces like fear of the unknown, loss of control, or perceived threats to job security.

To navigate resistance effectively, leaders should focus on communication and involvement. Transparently sharing the rationale for the change, its benefits, and its expected outcomes can help demystify the process and reduce anxieties. Encouraging open dialogue allows employees to voice their concerns and suggestions, providing valuable insights that can strengthen the change strategy and mitigate resistance.

Fostering employee engagement throughout the change process is critical. Leaders can achieve this by involving employees in planning and decision-making, creating cross-functional teams to work on change-related projects, and recognizing and celebrating early wins and contributions. This inclusive approach not only leverages the diverse skills and perspectives within the organization but also builds a collective commitment to the change. Moreover, training and development play a crucial role in preparing employees for the change. Providing opportunities for skill development and knowledge sharing can ease the transition, helping employees feel more competent and confident in their roles within the new organizational structure.

As the change is implemented, continuously monitoring the balance between driving and restraining forces allows leaders to make necessary adjustments, ensuring that the momentum towards the desired state is maintained. This might involve reinforcing successful strategies, addressing emerging challenges, or recalibrating the approach based on feedback and outcomes.

The successful application of Lewin's leadership styles and force field analysis to organizational change requires a dynamic and responsive leadership approach. By thoughtfully navigating resistance and actively fostering employee engagement, leaders can create an environment where change is not only accepted but embraced, leading to a stronger, more adaptable organization.

Choosing the appropriate leadership style to facilitate change processes is a nuanced decision that hinges on understanding the specific context and goals of the organization. Leaders must weigh various factors, including the nature of the change, the organization's culture, the readiness of employees, and the urgency of the situation, to select a leadership style that will most effectively guide the organization through the transition.

Contextual Considerations

- Nature of the Change: Transformational changes that fundamentally alter the organization's direction or strategy may benefit from a more democratic leadership style. This approach fosters buy-in and support by involving employees in the change process, ensuring their perspectives and concerns are addressed. Conversely, incremental changes or situations requiring swift action might necessitate a more autocratic style, where decisions are made quickly and directives are clear.

- Organizational Culture: The existing culture of an organization can significantly influence the choice of leadership style. In cultures that value autonomy and innovation, a laissez-faire approach might be effective, empowering employees to explore new ideas and solutions. In contrast, organizations with a hierarchical structure may respond better to autocratic or democratic styles, depending on the level of participation and engagement typically encouraged.

- Employee Readiness and Resistance: Understanding employees' readiness for change and their potential resistance is crucial. A democratic leadership style can be particularly effective in environments where resistance is anticipated, as it allows for dialogue, negotiation, and consensus-building. For teams that are more open and ready for change, a laissez-faire style might encourage creativity and ownership of the change process.

- Urgency and Complexity: The urgency of the change and its complexity also play a role in determining the leadership style. High-urgency situations, especially in crisis conditions, may require an autocratic approach to ensure rapid decision-making and implementation. In contrast, complex changes that impact many aspects of the organization and require careful consideration of diverse perspectives may benefit from a democratic approach, ensuring thorough analysis and buy-in.

Strategic Application

Leaders can strategically apply different leadership styles at various stages of the change process to address these contextual factors effectively. For instance, an autocratic style might be used to initiate a change quickly, followed by a shift to a democratic style to develop the change strategy with broad input. As the change is implemented, a laissez-faire approach could then empower employees to take ownership of new processes or innovations.

Adaptability and Flexibility

The key to successfully facilitating change processes lies in a leader's adaptability and flexibility. Leaders must be willing to shift their leadership style as circumstances evolve, remaining attuned to the organization's needs and employees' responses throughout the change process. This dynamic approach ensures that leadership remains effective across different phases of change, addressing challenges and leveraging opportunities as they arise.

The choice of leadership style in facilitating organizational change is a deliberate decision that requires a deep understanding of the specific context, goals, and dynamics of the organization. By thoughtfully selecting and adapting their leadership approach, leaders can navigate change more effectively, minimizing disruption and fostering a positive transition towards new organizational objectives.

**Relevance to Contemporary Leadership Practice**

Kurt Lewin's research, particularly his work on leadership styles, group dynamics, and the force field analysis model, remains profoundly relevant to contemporary leadership practice. His insights into human behavior, organizational change, and conflict resolution continue to offer valuable frameworks for leaders navigating the complexities of the modern workplace. In the areas of change management and conflict resolution, Lewin's theories provide actionable strategies that are as applicable today as they were when first introduced.

Change Management

In today's fast-paced and often unpredictable business environment, the ability to manage change effectively is a critical skill for leaders. Lewin's three-stage model of change—unfreezing, changing, and refreezing—outlines a process for implementing change that is both systematic and considerate of the human factors involved. This model emphasizes the importance of preparing organizations for change, implementing the change, and then solidifying the new state as the norm. It addresses the psychological resistance to change, offering leaders strategies for engaging and motivating teams through transitions. Lewin's force field analysis provides leaders with a tool to assess the driving and restraining forces impacting an organizational change initiative. By identifying and understanding these forces, leaders can develop targeted strategies to strengthen drivers of change and reduce barriers. This approach is particularly relevant in navigating the complexities of digital transformation, market shifts, and organizational restructuring, common challenges in contemporary business.

Conflict Resolution

Lewin's research on group dynamics and leadership styles also offers insights into conflict resolution within teams and organizations. His identification of autocratic, democratic, and laissez-faire leadership styles allows leaders to reflect on their approach to managing conflict. For example, a democratic leadership style, which fosters open communication and participation, can be particularly effective in resolving conflicts by ensuring all voices are heard and considered. This style aligns with modern emphases on inclusivity and collaborative problem-solving. His emphasis on the social aspects of group behavior—how individuals are influenced by the presence and expectations of others—highlights the importance of creating a culture where constructive conflict is seen as an opportunity for growth and innovation. By applying Lewin's principles, leaders can navigate conflicts more effectively, turning potential sources of friction into catalysts for team cohesion and creativity.

Contemporary Application

In applying Lewin's theories to contemporary challenges, leaders are equipped to handle the complexities of change management and conflict resolution with a deeper understanding of human behavior and organizational dynamics. Lewin's work encourages a balanced approach to leadership that considers both the task and the people involved, promoting strategies that are not only effective but also sustainable and respectful of the individuals impacted by change and conflict. Kurt Lewin's legacy in the field of social psychology continues to influence contemporary leadership practices significantly. His pioneering research provides a foundational understanding of how to lead effectively through change and conflict, offering timeless strategies for navigating the challenges of modern organizational life. As leaders face new and evolving challenges, Lewin's work remains a valuable resource, underscoring the importance of adaptability, empathy, and strategic thinking in effective leadership.

Kurt Lewin's foundational concepts in group dynamics and change management offer a rich theoretical base that can be integrated with modern theories and practices in leadership development, such as emotional intelligence and transformational leadership. This integration provides a comprehensive approach to leadership that combines the insights of social psychology with contemporary understandings of leadership effectiveness.

Integration with Emotional Intelligence

Emotional intelligence, which involves the ability to understand and manage one's own emotions and those of others, aligns closely with Lewin's emphasis on the psychological dimensions of leadership and group dynamics. Lewin's leadership styles—autocratic, democratic, and laissez-faire—can be enhanced by incorporating principles of emotional intelligence. For instance:

- Democratic leadership benefits significantly from emotional intelligence, particularly in the realms of empathy and social skills. Leaders who can empathize with team members' perspectives and manage emotions constructively can foster a more inclusive and participative environment, enhancing group cohesion and motivation.

- Autocratic leadership might be applied more effectively when tempered by emotional awareness. Even in situations requiring decisive leadership, understanding the emotional impact of decisions and communicating with sensitivity can mitigate potential negative effects on team morale.

- Laissez-faire leadership requires a high degree of emotional intelligence to recognize when autonomy is fostering innovation and when it may be leading to disengagement or confusion. Leaders must be attuned to the emotional cues of their team to provide support and direction as needed.

Integration with Transformational Leadership

Transformational leadership, which inspires followers to exceed their own self-interests for the good of the organization and to achieve higher levels of performance, also finds synergy with

Lewin's concepts. Transformational leaders, much like those employing Lewin's democratic style, focus on motivating and empowering followers, but they add layers of vision, inspiration, and personal development. Integrating Lewin's ideas with transformational leadership could involve:

- Incorporating Lewin's change management strategies—unfreezing, changing, and refreezing—into the transformational leader's efforts to inspire and implement organizational change. Transformational leaders can use Lewin's force field analysis to strategically map out the driving and restraining forces affecting change initiatives, tailoring their inspirational and motivational efforts to address these specific factors.

- Leveraging group dynamics to foster transformational change. Lewin's emphasis on understanding group behavior and the importance of facilitating effective group processes can help transformational leaders create environments that nurture creativity, innovation, and collective effort towards shared goals.

- Applying Lewin's leadership styles in a flexible manner, adapting to the needs of the situation and the development stage of the team. Transformational leaders can utilize aspects of autocratic leadership for quick decision-making when necessary, democratic leadership to engage and empower followers, and laissez-faire leadership to encourage independence and personal growth.

Integrating Lewin's concepts with emotional intelligence and transformational leadership provides a multidimensional approach to leadership development. This approach recognizes the complexity of leading in the modern world, where leaders must navigate not only the task and structural aspects of their roles but also the deeply human elements of motivation, emotion, and transformation. By drawing on the strengths of Lewin's theories and combining them with the insights offered by emotional intelligence and transformational leadership, leaders can develop more effective, adaptive, and holistic leadership practices.

Navigating change and conflict within organizations requires a nuanced understanding of leadership dynamics and the factors that drive or hinder organizational progress. Kurt Lewin's leadership styles and his force field analysis model provide valuable frameworks for leaders seeking to manage these complex processes effectively. By applying Lewin's concepts, leaders can develop strategies that not only address the immediate challenges of change and conflict but also foster a culture of adaptability and resilience.

Understanding and adapting leadership styles is crucial in navigating change and conflict. Leaders should assess the context and the specific needs of their organization to determine which style—autocratic, democratic, or laissez-faire—will be most effective. For instance, during the initial stages of a significant change, a more autocratic approach might be necessary to set clear directions and ensure quick decision-making. However, as the change progresses, transitioning to a democratic style can help in building consensus, encouraging participation, and ensuring that the voices of team members are heard. This shift not only facilitates smoother implementation of change but also helps in mitigating conflict by involving employees in the process, thereby increasing their commitment and reducing resistance.

Lewin's force field analysis is another powerful tool for leaders managing change and conflict. By identifying the driving forces that support the change and the restraining forces that oppose it, leaders can develop targeted interventions to strengthen positive drivers and address or reduce barriers. This might involve enhancing communication to clarify the benefits of the change, providing training and resources to ease the transition, or engaging in team-building activities to strengthen cohesion and address underlying conflicts.

Effective navigation of change also requires leaders to be proactive in managing conflict. Recognizing that conflict can be a natural byproduct of change, leaders should strive to address issues openly and constructively. Employing strategies such as active listening, mediation, and negotiation can help in resolving disputes and finding mutually beneficial solutions. Leaders should foster an environment where differing viewpoints are respected and where conflicts are viewed as opportunities for growth and improvement.

Leaders should emphasize the importance of flexibility and learning throughout the change process. Encouraging a culture of continuous improvement, where feedback is sought and valued, can help organizations adapt more effectively to change and overcome challenges. This approach not only supports the successful implementation of specific change initiatives but also builds a foundation for long-term adaptability and resilience.

Navigating change and conflict within organizations demands a strategic and adaptable leadership approach. By leveraging Lewin's leadership styles and force field analysis, leaders can develop comprehensive strategies that address both the structural and human dimensions of change. This holistic approach ensures that change initiatives are implemented successfully while also building a culture that values participation, adaptability, and continuous learning.

## Contemporary Applications and Case Studies

In today's fast-paced and complex organizational environments, the role of adaptive leadership has become increasingly critical. Adaptive leadership is about navigating uncertainty, leading through change, and fostering an environment where learning and innovation can thrive. Kurt Lewin's theories, particularly those related to leadership styles, group dynamics, and change management, provide a foundational framework for understanding and applying adaptive leadership in contemporary settings.

Adaptive Leadership and Lewin's Change Management

Lewin's three-stage model of change—unfreezing, change (moving), and refreezing—offers a blueprint for adaptive leadership. In a rapidly changing environment, leaders must continually engage in the unfreezing process, challenging the status quo and preparing the organization for change. This involves questioning existing beliefs and practices and encouraging openness to new ideas and ways of working. The change (moving) stage aligns with adaptive leadership's focus on experimentation and learning, as leaders and their teams explore new solutions and adapt to emerging challenges. Finally, the refreezing stage, in an adaptive context, is less about solidifying a new status quo and more about establishing a culture of continuous improvement and adaptability.

Lewin's Leadership Styles and Adaptability

Lewin's identification of autocratic, democratic, and laissez-faire leadership styles underscores the importance of adaptability in leadership approaches. Adaptive leaders recognize the need to flex their leadership style based on the situation, the needs of the team, and the specific challenges faced. For instance, in situations requiring rapid response or when clear direction is needed, an autocratic style may be temporarily adopted. However, to foster innovation, engagement, and collective problem-solving, shifting to a democratic style enables leaders to draw on the diverse perspectives and skills of their team. In environments where team members are highly skilled and motivated, a laissez-faire approach can empower individuals and encourage creativity and independence.

Group Dynamics and Adaptive Leadership

Lewin's work on group dynamics, including his force field analysis model, is particularly relevant for adaptive leadership. Understanding the driving and restraining forces affecting change enables leaders to more effectively navigate the complexities of organizational transformation. Adaptive leaders use this insight to engage stakeholders in identifying and addressing barriers to change while leveraging and amplifying positive drivers. This approach emphasizes the collaborative and participatory nature of adaptive leadership, where fostering a shared vision and collective effort is key to navigating uncertainty and achieving organizational goals.

Adaptive leadership, with its emphasis on flexibility, learning, and responsiveness, is well-suited to today's dynamic organizational environments. Drawing on Lewin's theories, adaptive leaders can better understand and navigate the processes of change and the dynamics of team behavior. By applying Lewin's insights into leadership styles and group dynamics, leaders can develop strategies that promote adaptability, resilience, and continuous improvement. In essence, Lewin's work offers valuable guidance for leaders seeking to navigate the complexities of modern organizational life, underscoring the importance of adaptability, engagement, and a deep understanding of the human aspects of change.

Let's examine a hypothetical case study inspired by common scenarios in contemporary organizations, illustrating the application of Kurt Lewin's adaptive leadership styles—autocratic, democratic, and laissez-faire—in managing a technology firm's transition to remote work due to unforeseen circumstances, such as a global pandemic.

Background

Global Tech, a mid-sized software development company, faced an urgent need to transition to a fully remote operation model as a response to a sudden global pandemic. The CEO, Alex, recognized the challenge of maintaining productivity, ensuring employee well-being, and sustaining innovation during this abrupt change.

Application of Lewin's Leadership Styles

1. Autocratic Leadership at the Outset

Initially, Alex adopted an autocratic leadership style to quickly implement the remote work policy. Recognizing the urgency of the situation, Alex made immediate decisions regarding remote work protocols, technology infrastructure upgrades, and communication channels. This approach ensured a swift and organized transition, addressing the critical need for business continuity.

2. Transitioning to Democratic Leadership

With the initial crisis managed, Alex shifted to a democratic leadership style to navigate the ongoing adjustments and improvements needed. Alex initiated regular virtual town hall meetings and created cross-functional teams to discuss challenges, gather feedback, and propose solutions for effective remote work. This participative approach fostered a sense of ownership among employees, encouraging collaboration and innovative problem-solving. It also allowed the team to contribute to refining work-from-home policies, balancing productivity with flexibility to accommodate diverse needs.

3. Incorporating Laissez-faire Leadership

As employees adjusted to the new remote work environment, Alex adopted a more laissez-faire approach in areas where teams showed high levels of self-motivation and competence. Recognizing the importance of trust and autonomy in driving innovation, Alex provided teams with the freedom to experiment with new project management tools and asynchronous work schedules. This hands-off leadership facilitated creativity and allowed teams to tailor their work processes to maximize efficiency and job satisfaction.

Outcomes

- Enhanced Productivity and Innovation: The adaptive leadership approach led to sustained, and in some areas improved, productivity levels. Teams felt empowered to innovate, leading to the development of new software features that better met customer needs during the pandemic.

- Increased Employee Satisfaction and Well-being: By involving employees in decision-making and giving them autonomy, Global Tech saw an increase in job satisfaction. The company also implemented new wellness programs based on employee feedback, addressing mental health and work-life balance concerns.

- Strengthened Organizational Resilience: The experience of adapting to remote work under Alex's adaptive leadership strengthened the company's resilience. Employees developed new skills, and the company culture became more flexible and responsive to change.

This case study illustrates the effectiveness of applying Lewin's adaptive leadership styles in a contemporary organizational setting. By skillfully transitioning between autocratic, democratic, and laissez-faire leadership based on the phase of change and team dynamics, Alex was able to guide Global Tech through a challenging transition, resulting in a stronger, more adaptable organization. This approach highlights the relevance of Lewin's theories in navigating the complexities of modern organizational challenges.

We provide below a three more hypothetical examples that showcase how leaders might successfully navigate complex change initiatives or resolve conflicts by applying Kurt Lewin's theories. These examples, while fictional, are inspired by common organizational scenarios and demonstrate the application of Lewin's leadership styles and change management principles.

1. Navigating a Merger in the Tech Industry

Sarah, the CEO of a mid-sized tech company, faces the challenge of merging with a smaller competitor to expand her company's market share and product offerings. She is aware of the potential for cultural clashes and resistance from employees on both sides.

Sarah starts with town hall meetings to discuss the merger's benefits and address concerns openly, using Lewin's unfreezing stage to prepare employees for change. Democratic Leadership: Recognizing the need for buy-in, Sarah employs a democratic leadership style, forming cross-functional teams from both companies to identify best practices and integrate systems and cultures smoothly. As the new combined culture begins to take shape, Sarah focuses on solidifying these changes through regular updates, celebrating wins, and embedding the new culture into policies and everyday practices.

2.  Introducing a New Product Line

Mike, a product manager at a consumer goods company, is tasked with leading his team through the development and launch of a new product line, a significant departure from the company's traditional offerings.

Initially, Mike uses an autocratic style to make quick decisions on budgets and timelines to kickstart the project. Shifting to a democratic approach, Mike involves his team in brainstorming sessions for product features and marketing strategies, fostering creativity and commitment. As the team gains momentum, Mike adopts a laissez-faire approach, giving team members autonomy to innovate and solve problems independently, fostering a sense of ownership and accountability.

3.  Overcoming Resistance to Digital Transformation

Linda, the IT director of a traditional publishing house, is tasked with leading a digital transformation initiative to modernize the company's operations. She anticipates significant resistance from a workforce accustomed to traditional methods.

Linda conducts a force field analysis to identify driving forces (e.g., market pressure, efficiency gains) and restraining forces (e.g., employee fear, lack of digital skills). Linda begins with an autocratic approach to quickly procure necessary digital tools and infrastructure. Recognizing the need for team support, she then transitions to a democratic leadership style, involving employees in training sessions and pilot projects to build competence and confidence. Throughout the process, she maintains open channels of communication, addressing concerns and celebrating milestones to motivate the team.

These examples illustrate how leaders can effectively apply Lewin's theories to navigate complex change initiatives and resolve conflicts. By skillfully adapting their leadership style to the needs of the situation and employing Lewin's change management principles, leaders can guide their teams through transitions smoothly, mitigate resistance, and achieve sustainable organizational change.

## Conclusion

Kurt Lewin's groundbreaking work has left an indelible mark on the fields of leadership and organizational psychology, offering insights and frameworks that continue to influence modern leadership practice. His pioneering research into group dynamics, leadership styles, and change management has provided leaders with valuable tools for navigating the complexities of organizational life. This chapter has explored Lewin's key contributions and their enduring relevance, highlighting how his theories can be applied to address contemporary challenges in leadership and change initiatives.

Lewin's leadership styles—autocratic, democratic, and laissez-faire—have offered a foundational understanding of how different approaches to leadership can impact group behavior and organizational outcomes. These styles underscore the importance of adaptability in leadership, encouraging leaders to adjust their approach based on the situation, goals, and needs of their teams. In today's ever-changing organizational environments, the ability to transition fluidly between leadership styles is crucial for effectively managing teams, fostering innovation, and navigating challenges.

Lewin's force field analysis model remains a powerful tool for understanding and managing organizational change. By identifying and analyzing the driving and restraining forces that impact change initiatives, leaders can develop targeted strategies to promote positive change and mitigate resistance. This model offers a structured approach to change management that is both strategic and empathetic, recognizing the importance of addressing human factors and emotions in the change process.

Lewin's three-stage model of change—unfreezing, changing, and refreezing—provides a practical roadmap for implementing change in organizations. This model emphasizes the need for thorough preparation, active engagement with the change process, and reinforcement of new behaviors and practices. It highlights the iterative nature of change, encouraging leaders to remain flexible and responsive to feedback as they guide their organizations through transitions.

The practical applications of Lewin's theories in modern leadership practice are vast. From enhancing team dynamics and resolving conflicts to leading transformative change initiatives, Lewin's insights help leaders understand the underlying psychological processes that influence organizational behavior. His work encourages a holistic approach to leadership, one that balances task achievement with the emotional and social needs of team members.

Kurt Lewin's contributions to leadership and organizational psychology have provided a lasting legacy that continues to inform and guide leaders across various industries and contexts. By applying Lewin's theories, leaders can navigate the complexities of organizational change with greater insight, empathy, and effectiveness. His work underscores the importance of understanding human behavior in organizational settings and offers a comprehensive framework for cultivating leadership that is both adaptive and transformative.

In the dynamic landscape of contemporary organizations, where change is constant and conflict inevitable, leaders are continually seeking effective strategies to navigate these challenges. Incorporating Kurt Lewin's insights into leadership approaches offers a robust foundation for managing these complexities with grace and effectiveness. Lewin's pioneering work in group dynamics, leadership styles, and change management provides not only a theoretical framework but also practical tools that can significantly enhance leadership practice, especially in times of transition and turmoil.

By embracing Lewin's contributions, leaders can equip themselves with the knowledge and skills needed to navigate the complexities of change and conflict with confidence and competence. This approach fosters a leadership style characterized by flexibility, empathy, and strategic acumen, qualities that are increasingly valuable in today's fast-paced and ever-evolving organizational environments. Leaders who incorporate Lewin's insights into their practice can expect to see not only enhanced organizational outcomes but also enriched personal growth and leadership development.

# Chapter 6: Manfred Kets de Vries and the Psychological Health of Leaders

Manfred Kets de Vries stands out as a pivotal figure in the intersection of psychoanalysis and leadership, bringing a profound depth to the understanding of leadership behavior through the lens of psychological health. With a distinguished career that melds the insights of psychoanalytic theory with the practicalities of management and leadership, Kets de Vries offers a unique perspective on the complexities of leading and managing organizations. His work illuminates the often-overlooked psychological underpinnings of leadership dynamics, providing invaluable insights into the human aspects of organizational life.

At the heart of Kets de Vries's contributions is his exploration of the psychological health of leaders. He delves into how leaders' mental and emotional well-being impacts their decision-making, their interactions with others, and ultimately, the performance and culture of their organizations. Kets de Vries's work challenges leaders to reflect on their own psychological makeup, encouraging a journey of self-awareness and growth that is crucial for effective leadership.

Another central theme in Kets de Vries's work is the dark side of leadership. He examines the behaviors and traits that, while often contributing to a leader's rise to power, can also lead to their downfall and negatively affect their organizations. This exploration includes issues such as narcissism, authoritarianism, and the inability to manage stress or failure. By shedding light on these aspects, Kets de Vries provides a cautionary tale on the potential pitfalls of unchecked leadership behavior.

Kets de Vries delves into the dynamics within leadership teams, highlighting the importance of emotional intelligence, trust, and collaboration in achieving organizational goals. He emphasizes the role of leaders in creating a psychologically safe environment that fosters creativity, innovation, and resilience among team members.

As this chapter unfolds, we will explore Manfred Kets de Vries's significant contributions to understanding the psychological aspects of leadership. By integrating psychoanalytic principles with leadership theory, Kets de Vries offers a comprehensive approach that enriches our understanding of what it means to lead effectively. Through his insights, leaders are invited to embark on a journey of personal and professional development, one that not only enhances their leadership capabilities but also promotes the well-being and success of their organizations.

**The Psychological Aspects of Leadership**

Manfred Kets de Vries's profound analysis of the psychological dimensions underlying leadership behaviors and styles presents a compelling narrative about how leaders' personal histories significantly shape their leadership approaches. Through his integration of psychoanalytic principles with leadership theory, Kets de Vries uncovers the deep psychological currents that influence leaders' actions, decision-making processes, and interactions with others.

A central aspect of his work is the concept that leaders' personal narratives—comprising their early life experiences, formative relationships, and pivotal moments—play a crucial role in defining their leadership style. These personal histories can manifest in various ways, from the leader's communication style and conflict resolution strategies to their motivation for power and their approach to risk-taking. He posits that unresolved issues from a leader's past can surface in the workplace, influencing their behavior in ways that may be unconscious to them but palpable to those they lead. For example, a leader who experienced a lack of control or instability during their upbringing may exhibit a need for dominance or a preference for highly structured environments. Conversely, leaders who received strong support and encouragement may be more inclined to adopt empowering and participative leadership styles.

The interplay between personal history and leadership approach is also evident in how leaders deal with stress, failure, and uncertainty. Kets de Vries highlights the importance of emotional resilience, which can be traced back to earlier life challenges and how they were navigated. Leaders who have developed coping mechanisms and a strong sense of self-efficacy are better equipped to handle the pressures of leadership and foster a positive organizational culture.

He emphasizes the role of self-awareness in mitigating the potentially negative impacts of one's personal history on leadership behavior. By engaging in self-reflection and possibly psychotherapy, leaders can gain insights into their psychological makeup, identifying patterns that may hinder their effectiveness. This process of introspection and growth allows leaders to transform their vulnerabilities into strengths, enhancing their ability to lead authentically and empathetically. Kets de Vries's analysis extends to the dynamics within leadership teams, illustrating how leaders' psychological traits influence team interactions and organizational outcomes. He advocates for creating psychologically healthy work environments where open communication, mutual respect, and emotional support prevail. Such environments enable teams to navigate challenges more effectively, innovate, and achieve their collective goals.

Manfred Kets de Vries's exploration of the psychological dimensions of leadership provides a nuanced understanding of the complex interplay between leaders' personal histories and their leadership approaches. By acknowledging and addressing these psychological underpinnings, leaders can foster more effective, resilient, and compassionate leadership, contributing to the overall health and success of their organizations.

His exploration into the unconscious factors that drive leadership decisions and the formation of organizational cultures reveals a profound understanding of the psychological depths influencing organizational life. His work illuminates how unconscious dynamics, often rooted in leaders' early experiences and inner conflicts, shape not only their decision-making processes but also the broader cultural and relational patterns within organizations.

Unconscious Drivers of Leadership Decisions

Kets de Vries posits that many leadership decisions, while seemingly rational on the surface, are significantly influenced by unconscious factors. These include deep-seated fears, desires, and motivations that leaders themselves may not be fully aware of. For instance, a leader's decision-making style—whether it is risk-averse or risk-seeking—may be unconsciously driven by an underlying need for security or a desire for recognition. Similarly, leaders' responses to stress, challenge, or conflict often reflect unconscious coping mechanisms developed in response to earlier life experiences.

The impact of these unconscious drivers is particularly evident in times of crisis or significant change when leaders' default behaviors and decision-making patterns come to the fore. Kets de Vries highlights the importance of self-awareness and emotional intelligence in recognizing and managing these unconscious influences. By engaging in reflective practices or seeking psychoanalytic support, leaders can uncover the roots of their unconscious biases and motivations, leading to more deliberate and effective decision-making.

Formation of Organizational Cultures

Kets de Vries extends his analysis to the realm of organizational culture, arguing that the unconscious dynamics of leaders play a crucial role in shaping the values, norms, and behaviors that define an organization. Leaders, through their actions, communication, and decision-making, serve as role models, transmitting their own psychological predispositions and unresolved conflicts to the organizational environment. This transmission can lead to the formation of organizational cultures that mirror the leader's unconscious dynamics, for better or worse. For example, a leader who operates from a place of insecurity or unresolved authority conflicts may unconsciously foster a culture of competition, fear, and power struggles. Conversely, a leader who has worked through such issues and developed a secure sense of self may cultivate an organizational culture characterized by trust, collaboration, and psychological safety.

He emphasizes the transformative potential of addressing these unconscious dynamics. Leaders who are willing to explore and understand their own psychological underpinnings can intentionally shape organizational cultures that promote health, resilience, and positive engagement. This involves creating spaces for open dialogue, encouraging emotional expression, and modeling behaviors that align with desired cultural values.

The insights into the unconscious factors driving leadership decisions and the formation of organizational cultures provide a compelling framework for understanding the psychological complexity of organizational life. By acknowledging the influence of unconscious dynamics, leaders can undertake the challenging yet rewarding work of personal development, leading to more insightful, compassionate, and effective leadership. In turn, this personal growth facilitates the creation of organizational cultures that not only support the fulfillment of business objectives but also contribute to the well-being and development of all members of the organization.

**The Dark Side of Leadership**

Manfred Kets de Vries's examination of the dark side of leadership delves into the traits and behaviors that, while potentially contributing to a leader's ascent, can also precipitate dysfunctional leadership and engender toxic organizational environments. This aspect of his work provides critical insights into how certain psychological patterns, when left unchecked, can undermine the health and success of organizations.

Traits and Behaviors Constituting the Dark Side: Kets de Vries identifies several traits and behaviors associated with the dark side of leadership, including narcissism, authoritarianism, Machiavellianism, and emotional volatility. These traits, while they may offer short-term advantages in terms of decisiveness or charisma, can lead to significant long-term issues:

- Narcissism: Leaders exhibiting narcissistic tendencies may possess a charismatic allure, driving vision and ambition. However, their need for admiration and sense of entitlement can result in a lack of empathy, exploitation of others, and a disregard for the collaborative aspects of leadership. This can stifle dissent, discourage genuine feedback, and promote a culture of conformity.

- Authoritarianism: Authoritarian leaders, who prioritize control and obedience, may initially establish order and direction. Yet, over time, this leadership style can suppress creativity, decrease employee engagement, and foster a climate of fear and resentment.

- Machiavellianism: Leaders who manipulate and deceive to achieve their ends can create an environment of mistrust and paranoia, undermining team cohesion and ethical standards.

- Emotional Volatility: Leaders lacking emotional regulation may react impulsively to challenges, leading to inconsistent decision-making and creating a stressful, unpredictable work environment.

Consequences of Dysfunctional Leadership: The presence of these dark traits in leadership can lead to several dysfunctional outcomes within organizations:

- Erosion of Trust: Toxic leadership erodes the foundation of trust necessary for effective teamwork and collaboration, leading to a breakdown in communication and organizational cohesion.

- Diminished Morale and Well-being: The stress and negativity associated with toxic leadership can significantly impact employees' morale and mental health, leading to higher turnover rates and decreased productivity.

- Ethical Breaches: A toxic leader's disregard for ethical norms can permeate the organization, leading to unethical practices and damaging the organization's reputation and legal standing.

Mitigating the Dark Side

Kets de Vries suggests that awareness and intervention are key to mitigating the dark side of leadership. Leaders themselves must engage in self-reflection and seek feedback to become aware of their potentially destructive patterns. Organizations can also play a crucial role by fostering a culture that values psychological health, ethical behavior, and transparent communication. This includes providing resources for leader development, establishing checks and balances to distribute power, and encouraging a culture where feedback and dialogue are valued.

He highlights the importance of psychoanalytic approaches in executive coaching and leadership development programs to address and transform these destructive patterns. By exploring the underlying psychological roots of their behaviors, leaders can develop healthier ways of relating to others and exercising their leadership roles. His exploration of the dark side of leadership serves as a vital reminder of the complex interplay between psychology and leadership effectiveness. Understanding and addressing the dark traits and behaviors in leadership is crucial for cultivating healthy, resilient, and ethically grounded organizational environments.

The exploration of the dark side of leadership through psychoanalytic theory sheds light on the complex psychological origins and manifestations of traits that can lead to dysfunctional leadership and toxic organizational environments. This theoretical perspective delves into how unresolved issues and conflicts from early childhood experiences shape personality development and influence leadership behavior in adulthood.

Understanding the origins and manifestations of these traits through psychoanalytic theory underscores the importance of self-awareness and emotional intelligence in leadership. It highlights the necessity for leaders to engage in deep introspection, seek constructive feedback, and consider psychoanalytic therapy or coaching to address these underlying issues. By confronting and working through these dark-side traits, leaders can cultivate healthier ways of leading, enhancing their effectiveness and positively influencing organizational culture.

**Leadership Teams Dynamics**

Manfred Kets de Vries's observations on the dynamics of leadership teams delve into the intricate web of unconscious processes, such as projection and transference, that underpin team interactions and influence decision-making. His work offers a nuanced understanding of how these psychological mechanisms can shape the relational dynamics within teams, potentially affecting their cohesion, efficiency, and overall performance.

Projection in Team Dynamics

Projection, a defense mechanism where individuals attribute their own unacceptable thoughts, feelings, or motives to another person, plays a significant role in team interactions. Kets de Vries highlights how leaders and team members might project their insecurities, fears, or desires onto others, leading to misunderstandings and conflicts that are not rooted in actual differences or issues but in the internal conflicts of the individuals involved. For instance, a leader who is insecure about their competence may perceive team members' questions or suggestions as criticisms or challenges to their authority, leading to defensive behaviors that stifle open communication and collaboration.

Transference in Leadership and Team Interactions

Transference, the redirection of feelings and desires from one person to another, especially from earlier relationships onto a present person, significantly impacts leadership and team dynamics. Kets de Vries points out that team members may transfer feelings associated with parental figures or past authority figures onto the leader, affecting their expectations, reactions, and interactions within the team. This can manifest in idealization of the leader, where team members expect unattainable levels of guidance and protection, or in unwarranted rebellion against the leader's authority, mirroring unresolved conflicts with parental figures.

Decision-Making Influences

These unconscious processes can significantly influence team decision-making. Projection can lead to decision-making that is more about alleviating individual anxieties than about addressing the actual challenges or opportunities the team faces. Transference can skew the team's dynamics, with decisions either overly influenced by the desire to please or rebel against the leader, rather than grounded in rational analysis and collective wisdom.

Mitigating Unconscious Influences

Kets de Vries suggests that awareness and reflection are key to mitigating the impact of these unconscious processes on team dynamics. Leaders can foster an environment that encourages open communication and reflection, helping team members become aware of and address their projections and transferences. This includes creating spaces where feedback is shared constructively, and personal reflections are encouraged as part of the team's culture.

He emphasizes the role of leadership in modeling self-awareness and emotional intelligence. By openly addressing their own tendencies towards projection and transference, leaders can set a precedent for transparency and psychological safety within the team. This approach not only mitigates the negative impact of unconscious processes on team interactions and decision-making but also enhances the team's cohesion, adaptability, and resilience.

Mitigating the unconscious influences on leadership teams, as highlighted by Manfred Kets de Vries, involves a deliberate and nuanced approach that addresses the intricate psychological underpinnings of team dynamics. This process requires a deep dive into self-awareness, open communication, and the fostering of a psychologically safe environment where these unconscious processes can be recognized, understood, and managed.

Fostering Self-Awareness and Emotional Intelligence

A critical step in mitigating unconscious influences is the cultivation of self-awareness and emotional intelligence among leaders and team members. This involves individuals engaging in introspection and reflection to understand their own biases, fears, and motivations that may be contributing to projection and transference within the team. Leaders can facilitate this process by encouraging participation in workshops, training sessions, and coaching that focus on emotional intelligence skills, such as empathy, self-regulation, and social awareness. By developing a deeper understanding of oneself, individuals are better equipped to recognize when their actions or reactions are being driven by unconscious processes rather than objective reality.

Creating Spaces for Open Communication

Open and honest communication is essential for addressing and mitigating the impact of unconscious influences on team dynamics. Leaders should strive to create an environment where team members feel safe to express their thoughts, feelings, and concerns without fear of judgment or retribution. This can be achieved through regular team meetings dedicated to reflection and feedback, where individuals are encouraged to share their experiences and perceptions openly. Such forums allow team members to surface and discuss instances where projection or transference may be affecting their interactions, providing an opportunity for collective understanding and resolution.

## Establishing Psychological Safety

Psychological safety, a state in which individuals feel comfortable taking interpersonal risks, is paramount for mitigating unconscious influences. Leaders play a key role in establishing and maintaining this safety by modeling vulnerability, acknowledging their own mistakes and limitations, and responding to team members' contributions with respect and appreciation. When team members feel psychologically safe, they are more likely to engage in constructive conflict, explore their unconscious motivations, and challenge their assumptions and biases. This environment supports the team in navigating complex emotional undercurrents and facilitates more effective collaboration and decision-making.

## Engaging in Collective Reflection

Collective reflection sessions, where the team as a whole engages in examining their dynamics, can be powerful in bringing unconscious influences to light. These sessions can be guided by external facilitators, such as coaches or psychologists, who can help the team explore underlying emotional currents and relational patterns. Through guided discussions, role-playing, and other reflective practices, teams can develop a shared understanding of how unconscious processes are impacting their work together and devise strategies for addressing these challenges.

## Commitment to Ongoing Development

Mitigating unconscious influences is not a one-time effort but requires a commitment to ongoing personal and collective development. Leaders should foster a culture of continuous learning, where there is regular investment in personal development, team-building activities, and professional growth opportunities that address the psychological aspects of working in teams. This commitment ensures that the team remains vigilant and responsive to the subtle ways in which unconscious dynamics can influence their interactions and decisions.

By delving deeper into the strategies for mitigating unconscious influences, leadership teams can enhance their cohesion, creativity, and effectiveness. Manfred Kets de Vries's insights into these psychological dynamics offer a roadmap for leaders seeking to cultivate more conscious, reflective, and resilient teams capable of navigating the complexities of organizational life.

## Personality Disorders and Emotional Health in Organizational Life

Manfred Kets de Vries's work on the intersection of psychoanalysis and organizational behavior provides insightful analyses into how personality disorders and emotional health issues among leaders can profoundly affect organizational performance and culture. His approach underscores the complex ways in which the psychological well-being of leaders intertwines with the dynamics of the organizations they lead, shaping everything from day-to-day operations to long-term strategic directions.

Impact on Organizational Performance

Kets de Vries points out that leaders with personality disorders or unresolved emotional health issues can significantly impact an organization's performance. These impacts manifest in various ways, depending on the specific personality disorders or emotional challenges at play. For instance, leaders with narcissistic traits may push their organizations to pursue grandiose projects without a realistic assessment of risks and benefits, potentially jeopardizing the organization's stability. Alternatively, leaders struggling with anxiety disorders might avoid making critical decisions, leading to stagnation and lost opportunities.

The ripple effects of such leadership behaviors can lead to an environment where short-term gains are pursued at the expense of long-term sustainability. Furthermore, the decision-making process can become skewed, favoring the leader's emotional needs over the organization's strategic objectives. This misalignment can result in inefficient resource allocation, misdirected efforts, and ultimately, suboptimal organizational performance.

Effect on Organizational Culture

The emotional health and personality of leaders also play a pivotal role in shaping organizational culture. Leaders set the tone for the workplace environment, and their behaviors, values, and attitudes are often mirrored by their employees. Leaders with personality disorders may create a culture of fear, uncertainty, and competition rather than collaboration. For example, an organization led by a person with a borderline personality disorder might experience high levels of volatility, affecting employees' sense of security and well-being.

Kets de Vries highlights how such leaders can foster a culture where unhealthy behaviors are normalized, such as excessive risk-taking, unethical practices, or disregard for work-life balance. This normalization can lead to a toxic workplace environment where stress, burnout, and turnover are high, and employee engagement and satisfaction are low.

Strategies for Addressing These Issues

He advocates for a proactive approach to addressing the impact of personality disorders and emotional health issues in organizational settings. This approach involves several key strategies:

1. Leadership Development Programs: Implementing leadership development programs that include components of self-awareness, emotional intelligence, and mental health. Such programs can help leaders recognize their own behavioral patterns and their impact on the organization.

2. Executive Coaching and Psychotherapy: Encouraging leaders to engage in executive coaching or psychotherapy, especially those designed to address psychological issues. These interventions can provide leaders with the tools to manage

their emotional health more effectively and make more balanced decisions.

3. Cultivating a Supportive Culture: Building an organizational culture that prioritizes mental health and well-being, offering support systems such as counseling services, mental health days, and stress management programs.

4. Promoting Openness and Vulnerability: Encouraging a culture where openness and vulnerability are valued, enabling leaders and employees alike to share their challenges and support each other in addressing them.

By examining the intricate relationship between leaders' psychological well-being and organizational dynamics, Kets de Vries offers valuable insights into creating healthier, more resilient organizations. Addressing the emotional health issues and personality disorders of leaders not only benefits the individuals involved but also enhances organizational performance and cultivates a positive, supportive culture.

Recognizing and addressing mental health issues in the workplace is crucial for preventing negative outcomes and promoting a healthy organizational climate. Mental health challenges, if left unaddressed, can lead to decreased productivity, increased absenteeism, and a higher turnover rate, significantly impacting an organization's performance and culture. Beyond these direct impacts, the presence of unaddressed mental health issues can erode the foundation of trust and safety that is essential for effective teamwork and collaboration.

The importance of tackling mental health issues extends to fostering an inclusive and supportive workplace environment where all employees feel valued and understood. Creating such an environment not only enhances employee well-being but also boosts engagement and loyalty, contributing to a more resilient and adaptable organization. Moreover, a culture that prioritizes mental health can serve as a competitive advantage, attracting top talent who value supportive and progressive workplace policies.

Addressing mental health in the workplace requires a multifaceted approach. It involves developing comprehensive policies that support mental health, including access to counseling services, flexible work arrangements, and initiatives aimed at reducing workplace stress. Training for managers and leaders on recognizing signs of mental distress and providing appropriate support is also essential. Such training can equip them with the skills needed to navigate sensitive conversations and to act swiftly and compassionately when employees are struggling.

Normalizing discussions about mental health and challenging the stigma associated with mental illness are critical steps towards creating a more open and supportive workplace culture. This can be achieved through awareness campaigns, mental health days, and by leaders sharing their own experiences with mental health challenges, thereby modeling openness and vulnerability.

The proactive recognition and addressing of mental health issues underscore an organization's commitment to its most valuable asset—its people. By investing in mental health initiatives, organizations not only prevent negative outcomes but also promote a culture of health, well-being, and mutual respect. This not only benefits individual employees but also contributes to the creation of a more vibrant, productive, and innovative organizational climate, where everyone can thrive.

**Fostering Psychological Insight and Emotional Health**

Enhancing psychological insight and emotional health among leaders is fundamental to fostering effective leadership and a positive organizational culture. Drawing on Manfred Kets de Vries's recommendations, several strategies can be employed to support leaders in this endeavor, focusing on reflective practice, coaching, and psychotherapy. These strategies aim to deepen leaders' self-awareness, improve their emotional regulation, and equip them with the skills needed to manage the complexities of organizational life in a healthy and productive manner.

Encouraging leaders to engage in reflective practice is a powerful strategy for enhancing psychological insight. This involves setting aside regular time for introspection and journaling, where leaders can contemplate their actions, reactions, and the motivations behind them. Reflective practice allows leaders to identify patterns in their behavior, understand their emotional triggers, and gain insights into how their personal history influences their leadership style. By fostering a habit of reflection, leaders can become more mindful of their impact on others and make more conscious choices in their interactions and decision-making processes.

For leaders facing more significant emotional health challenges or those interested in a deeper exploration of their psychological underpinnings, psychotherapy can be an invaluable resource. Psychotherapy provides a safe and confidential space for leaders to address unresolved issues, work through emotional difficulties, and explore aspects of their personality that influence their leadership. Kets de Vries points out that psychotherapy, especially when focused on issues relevant to leadership and organizational dynamics, can lead to profound personal growth and transformation, enabling leaders to lead with greater authenticity, compassion, and resilience.

Beyond individual efforts, organizations play a crucial role in supporting leaders' psychological insight and emotional health. This can be achieved by fostering a culture that values continuous learning, self-improvement, and mental well-being. Organizations can provide resources and opportunities for leaders to engage in reflective practice, coaching, and psychotherapy. Additionally, promoting open dialogues about mental health, offering workshops on emotional intelligence and stress management, and encouraging a balanced approach to work and life are essential components of a supportive environment.

By implementing these strategies, leaders can enhance their psychological insight and emotional health, leading to more effective leadership and healthier organizational climates. Kets de Vries's work underscores the importance of addressing the psychological dimensions of leadership, highlighting that the well-being of leaders is intrinsically linked to the well-being of the organizations they lead.

Executive coaching and leadership development programs play a pivotal role in facilitating leaders' personal growth and emotional well-being, serving as essential tools for enhancing leadership effectiveness and fostering a healthy organizational culture. These programs, when thoughtfully designed and implemented, provide leaders with the insights, skills, and strategies needed to navigate the complexities of modern organizational life with greater self-awareness, resilience, and empathy.

Executive coaching offers a personalized, reflective space for leaders to explore their leadership style, behaviors, and the underlying motivations that drive them. This one-on-one relationship with a coach allows for deep dives into personal challenges and areas for growth, making it a powerful catalyst for transformation. Coaches can help leaders identify and work through emotional and psychological barriers that may be hindering their effectiveness, such as fear of failure, difficulty with conflict management, or challenges in work-life balance. Through targeted questions and reflective exercises, coaches encourage leaders to gain new perspectives on their experiences, fostering a deeper understanding of themselves and their impact on others. This process not only enhances leaders' emotional well-being but also equips them with the emotional intelligence skills critical for leading diverse and dynamic teams.

Leadership development programs offer structured opportunities for leaders to engage with concepts and practices that promote emotional well-being and effective leadership. These programs often cover topics such as emotional intelligence, stress management, communication skills, and team dynamics, providing a comprehensive toolkit for leaders to draw upon. Importantly, these programs can also introduce leaders to the importance of psychological health in leadership, exploring how factors like mental well-being, mindfulness, and self-care contribute to leadership success.

These development programs can foster a community of learning among leaders, creating a supportive network where experiences, challenges, and insights can be shared. This communal aspect can reduce the isolation often felt in leadership roles, reminding leaders that they are not alone in their experiences. It also allows for the sharing of strategies and solutions that have been effective in addressing similar challenges, enriching the learning experience.

Drawing on psychoanalytic insights, as Manfred Kets de Vries often does, can add a rich layer of depth to executive coaching and leadership development programs. By exploring the unconscious drivers of behavior, leaders can uncover the root causes of their challenges, leading to more lasting and meaningful change. This approach can help leaders develop greater empathy for themselves and others, improve their relationships, and foster a more inclusive and supportive organizational culture.

The role of executive coaching and leadership development programs in promoting leaders' personal growth and emotional well-being is indispensable. By providing the space, tools, and support for self-exploration and learning, these programs enable leaders to navigate their roles with greater confidence, compassion, and clarity. As leaders become more attuned to their own psychological needs and those of their teams, they can create healthier, more resilient organizations capable of thriving in an ever-changing world.

**Creating Psychologically Healthy Organizations**

Creating psychologically healthy organizations is a multifaceted endeavor that requires leaders to apply a deep understanding of human behavior, as illuminated by Manfred Kets de Vries's principles. By fostering environments that prioritize mental health, emotional intelligence, and constructive interpersonal dynamics, leaders can enhance employee well-being, engagement, and productivity. This process involves recognizing the inherent value of psychological health in the workplace and implementing strategies that reflect this understanding.

Leaders can begin by embedding psychological health into the organization's core values, ensuring that policies, practices, and leadership behaviors consistently reflect a commitment to supporting mental well-being. This might include offering access to mental health resources, such as counseling services or stress management programs, and creating policies that encourage work-life balance, such as flexible working hours and remote work options.

Communication plays a crucial role in creating psychologically healthy organizations. Leaders should strive to establish open lines of communication, where employees feel safe to express their thoughts, feelings, and concerns without fear of judgment or reprisal. This openness can be facilitated through regular check-ins, feedback sessions, and forums for discussing mental health and well-being. By modeling vulnerability and empathy in their communication, leaders can cultivate a culture of trust and psychological safety, where employees are encouraged to support one another and collaborate effectively.

Kets de Vries emphasizes the importance of reflective practice and self-awareness for leaders. By engaging in self-reflection and seeking feedback on their leadership style and its impact on others, leaders can identify and address their own behaviors that may be contributing to a less than optimal organizational climate. This reflective practice can extend to the entire organization, encouraging a culture of continuous learning and development where everyone is committed to personal and professional growth. In addition to these internal strategies, leaders can foster psychologically healthy environments by promoting diversity, equity, and inclusion within the organization. Recognizing and valuing the unique backgrounds, experiences, and perspectives of all employees can enhance a sense of belonging and contribute to a richer, more dynamic organizational culture. This inclusivity extends to recognizing and accommodating the different ways in which employees may experience and cope with mental health challenges, ensuring that the workplace is supportive of all individuals.

Kets de Vries highlights the role of executive coaching and leadership development programs in supporting leaders as they navigate the complexities of creating psychologically healthy organizations. Through coaching and development programs, leaders can gain insights into their leadership approach, explore new strategies for enhancing psychological health in the workplace, and develop the skills necessary to lead with compassion, empathy, and effectiveness. By applying Kets de Vries's principles, leaders can cultivate psychologically healthy organizational environments that not only support employee well-being but also drive engagement and productivity. This holistic approach recognizes that the health of an organization is intrinsically linked to the mental and emotional well-being of its people, underscoring the critical role of psychological health in achieving organizational success.

Emotionally intelligent leadership and the creation of supportive, resilient organizational cultures offer a myriad of benefits that extend across all levels of an organization, enhancing its capacity to navigate challenges, foster innovation, and sustain growth. By prioritizing emotional intelligence (EI) in leadership practices, organizations can cultivate environments where empathy, self-awareness, and effective communication are at the forefront, leading to a host of positive outcomes.

Emotionally intelligent leaders excel in understanding and managing their own emotions and recognizing and influencing the emotions of others. This ability fosters clear, empathetic communication and strengthens interpersonal relationships within the team. When leaders communicate with empathy and openness, it encourages a culture where feedback is shared constructively, and diverse perspectives are valued. This environment supports more effective collaboration, as team members feel heard and respected, leading to increased creativity and problem-solving capabilities.

Leaders who exhibit emotional intelligence are adept at creating a work environment that prioritizes the well-being of employees. By recognizing the signs of stress or burnout and responding with support and flexibility, emotionally intelligent leaders can address potential issues before they escalate. This attentiveness to employee well-being not only enhances individual satisfaction and work-life balance but also boosts overall engagement. Engaged employees are more committed, productive, and likely to contribute positively to the organizational culture, driving success and innovation.

A key component of emotional intelligence is the ability to manage and adapt to change effectively. Emotionally intelligent leaders can navigate the complexities of organizational change with a calm and focused approach, guiding their teams through transitions with clarity and assurance. This adaptability fosters a culture of resilience, where challenges are viewed as opportunities for growth and learning. Organizations with resilient cultures are better equipped to withstand market fluctuations, technological advancements, and other external pressures, maintaining a competitive edge.

Emotionally intelligent leadership plays a crucial role in establishing trust and psychological safety within an organization. Leaders who demonstrate authenticity, vulnerability, and consistency in their actions cultivate an atmosphere where employees feel safe to take risks, voice their opinions, and admit mistakes. This psychological safety is foundational to fostering a culture of innovation, as it encourages experimentation and learning from failure without fear of retribution. Trust and psychological safety also contribute to stronger team cohesion and loyalty, further enhancing organizational performance.

The benefits of emotionally intelligent leadership and supportive, resilient organizational cultures contribute to the overall success and sustainability of an organization. By creating an environment where employees are engaged, supported, and motivated, organizations can achieve higher levels of performance, customer satisfaction, and employee retention. Emotionally intelligent leadership practices align with the growing emphasis on corporate social responsibility and ethical business practices, appealing to consumers, investors, and potential employees alike.

The integration of emotional intelligence into leadership practices and the cultivation of supportive, resilient organizational cultures yield significant benefits. These include improved communication and collaboration, enhanced employee well-being and engagement, increased adaptability and resilience, the establishment of trust and psychological safety, and ultimately, the driving of organizational success and sustainability.

## Conclusion

Manfred Kets de Vries's contributions to the field of leadership and organizational behavior offer profound insights into the psychological health of leaders and its cascading effects on leadership practice and organizational life. Through his extensive research and application of psychoanalytic principles, Kets de Vries has illuminated the complex interplay between a leader's inner world and their external effectiveness in leading organizations.

His work underscores the significance of emotional intelligence, self-awareness, and reflective practice in effective leadership. He posits that the journey towards effective leadership is deeply personal, requiring leaders to confront and understand their own psychological makeup. This process involves recognizing and addressing personal vulnerabilities, biases, and unconscious motivations, which, if left unchecked, can lead to dysfunctional leadership behaviors and negatively impact organizational culture.

A central theme in Kets de Vries's scholarship is the concept of the "inner theater" of leaders, a metaphorical space where personal history, fantasies, fears, and aspirations play out. He suggests that leaders' ability to engage with their inner theater through reflective practice and psychoanalytic exploration can lead to transformative personal growth and more authentic leadership. This introspective journey not only enhances leaders' emotional well-being but also equips them with the empathy, resilience, and emotional agility needed to navigate the complexities of modern organizational environments. Kets de Vries has explored the dark side of leadership, shedding light on how personality disorders and unresolved emotional issues can manifest as toxic leadership behaviors, contributing to unhealthy organizational climates. His work provides valuable strategies for identifying and mitigating these destructive patterns, advocating for a holistic approach to leadership development that encompasses mental health and emotional well-being.

The implications of Kets de Vries's work for leadership practice and organizational life are far-reaching. By prioritizing the psychological health of leaders, organizations can foster more supportive, resilient, and adaptive cultures. This focus on emotional health encourages a leadership style that is more inclusive, empathetic, and responsive to the needs of employees, promoting a positive organizational climate where trust, innovation, and collaboration thrive.

Manfred Kets de Vries's contributions offer a rich and nuanced understanding of the psychological underpinnings of leadership. His emphasis on the emotional and psychological well-being of leaders challenges conventional notions of leadership and provides a comprehensive framework for cultivating effective, emotionally intelligent leadership practices that can drive organizational success and foster healthy workplace environments.

Addressing the psychological dimensions of leadership is not merely an enhancement to leadership effectiveness but a fundamental necessity for nurturing well-being, ethical grounding, and sustainable success within organizations. The insights drawn from the work of scholars like Manfred Kets de Vries illuminate the profound impact of psychological health on leadership and organizational dynamics. Reflecting on this importance reveals several key areas where the psychological underpinnings of leadership play a crucial role. The effectiveness of leaders is deeply intertwined with their psychological well-being. Leaders who engage with their psychological dimensions are better equipped to manage stress, make balanced decisions, and maintain resilience in the face of challenges. This self-awareness enables leaders to navigate the complexities of their roles with greater clarity and focus, directly influencing their ability to inspire, motivate, and guide their teams toward shared goals.

The well-being of teams and the broader organizational climate are significantly affected by the emotional health of leaders. Leaders who are attentive to their psychological needs and those of their team members create environments where openness, trust, and mutual respect flourish. This attention to emotional well-being fosters a supportive culture that can enhance team cohesion, employee satisfaction, and organizational loyalty. By prioritizing psychological health, leaders can mitigate the risks of burnout and disengagement, contributing to a more vibrant and resilient workforce.

The ethical grounding of leaders is also closely linked to their psychological insight. A deep understanding of one's motivations, biases, and values—gained through reflection and exploration of the psychological self—serves as a moral compass, guiding leaders in making principled decisions. This ethical clarity is crucial for navigating the moral complexities and dilemmas that leaders frequently encounter. Leaders who are grounded in a strong sense of self and ethical awareness are more likely to act with integrity, fostering a culture of ethical behavior and accountability within their organizations.

Addressing the psychological dimensions of leadership has far-reaching implications for leadership development and succession planning. By incorporating psychological insights into leadership training and development programs, organizations can cultivate a pipeline of emotionally intelligent, self-aware, and ethically minded leaders. This investment in the psychological development of leaders not only enhances individual leader effectiveness but also ensures the long-term health and success of the organization.

The importance of addressing the psychological dimensions of leadership cannot be overstated. It is a critical factor in enhancing leadership effectiveness, ensuring the well-being of teams, and maintaining ethical standards within organizations. Leaders who embrace this aspect of their development are better prepared to lead with compassion, vision, and integrity, creating organizational cultures that are not only successful but also humane and ethically responsible.

Leaders and organizations stand at a critical juncture where prioritizing psychological insight and emotional health is not just beneficial but foundational to achieving leadership excellence and organizational success. In an era marked by rapid change, complexity, and an increasing understanding of the human aspects of work, the call to integrate psychological well-being into the fabric of organizational life has never been more pressing. Leaders, as the architects of organizational culture and the catalysts of change, have a unique opportunity and responsibility to champion this cause. By valuing and actively promoting psychological insight, leaders can unlock deeper levels of self-awareness, empathy, and resilience, not only within themselves but also among their teams. This journey begins with a commitment to personal growth, where leaders embrace the vulnerability of introspection and the courage to confront and transform their limitations.

Organizations, for their part, must create environments that support and nurture this psychological exploration. This involves establishing policies, practices, and resources that encourage mental health awareness, provide access to mental health support, and cultivate a culture of continuous learning and emotional intelligence. By doing so, organizations not only invest in the well-being of their employees but also lay the groundwork for a more adaptive, innovative, and sustainable future.

The benefits of prioritizing psychological insight and emotional health are manifold. Leaders who are emotionally healthy and psychologically insightful foster trust, creativity, and engagement within their teams. They navigate challenges with greater agility and make decisions that are not only effective but also compassionate and ethically sound. Moreover, organizations that prioritize these values are better positioned to attract and retain top talent, enhance their reputation, and achieve long-term success.

Encouraging leaders and organizations to prioritize psychological insight and emotional health is a call to action for a more humane and effective approach to leadership and organizational excellence. It is an invitation to embark on a transformative journey that not only elevates the individual leader but also uplifts the entire organization. By committing to this path, leaders and organizations can create a legacy of positive impact, resilience, and shared success that resonates far beyond the confines of the workplace.

The integration of psychological insight and emotional health into leadership and organizational practices is not just a strategic advantage but a moral imperative. It is time for leaders and organizations to embrace this holistic approach, recognizing that the true measure of their success is not just in the results they achieve but in the well-being of the people who make those results possible.

# Conclusion

This book has embarked on a profound journey through the advanced psychoanalytic concepts applied to leadership, weaving through the seminal works of Carl Jung, Alfred Adler, Erik Erikson, Wilfred Bion, Kurt Lewin, and Manfred Kets de Vries. Each theorist has contributed uniquely to our understanding of leadership dynamics, offering insights that stretch far beyond conventional leadership discourse to touch on the deeper, often unconscious aspects of leadership practice and organizational life.

From Carl Jung, we've explored the concept of archetypes and the collective unconscious, revealing how leadership personas can be influenced by universal patterns of human experience. Jung's work illuminates the symbolic dimensions of leadership, encouraging leaders to reflect on the archetypal roles they embody and how these roles resonate within their organizational cultures. Alfred Adler introduced us to the notions of striving for superiority and the importance of social interest. His theories shed light on the motivational forces driving leaders and how a balance between personal ambition and community welfare can lead to more collaborative and effective leadership.

Erik Erikson's stages of psychosocial development provided a framework for understanding the evolution of leadership identities over the lifespan. Erikson's work emphasizes the importance of navigating each developmental stage successfully to cultivate qualities essential for leadership, such as trust, autonomy, and integrity. Wilfred Bion's insights into group dynamics and the unconscious processes within teams offer valuable perspectives on the emotional undercurrents that influence team cohesion, decision-making, and organizational culture. Bion's concepts of basic assumption theory and the work group model highlight the leader's role in managing and containing group anxieties.

Kurt Lewin's research on leadership styles and group dynamics, grounded in psychological principles, underscores the impact of different leadership approaches on group behavior and organizational change. Lewin's force field analysis further enriches our understanding of the complexities involved in navigating organizational transformations. Manfred Kets de Vries brings a psychoanalytic lens to the emotional health of leaders, exploring how unresolved psychological issues can manifest as dysfunctional leadership behaviors. His work advocates for a more introspective approach to leadership development, emphasizing the need for leaders to engage in reflective practice and seek psychotherapeutic support when necessary.

Together, these theorists paint a comprehensive picture of the multifaceted implications of psychoanalytic theory for understanding leadership dynamics. They underscore the significance of unconscious processes, the developmental pathways that shape leadership personalities, and the critical role of emotional health in fostering effective, ethical, and resilient leaders and organizations.

As we reflect on these insights, it becomes clear that the journey toward effective leadership and organizational excellence is as much about inward exploration and psychological growth as it is about outward strategy and execution. By embracing the complexities of human psychology, leaders can cultivate deeper self-awareness, foster more meaningful connections with their teams, and build organizations that thrive on innovation, collaboration, and shared purpose.

**The Impact on Leadership Development**

The exploration of psychoanalytic concepts within the realm of leadership development marks a significant departure from traditional models, introducing depth and complexity that offer a more nuanced understanding of leadership behavior and effectiveness. This enriched perspective acknowledges the multifaceted nature of leadership, emphasizing the role of unconscious processes, emotional health, and psychological development alongside strategic acumen and decision-making skills.

Integrating psychoanalytic concepts into leadership development challenges the notion that effective leadership is solely the product of surface-level competencies and behaviors. Instead, it posits that true leadership effectiveness stems from a deep understanding of oneself and others, achieved through introspection and the exploration of one's psychological underpinnings. This approach encourages leaders to confront and understand their motivations, fears, and biases, recognizing how these elements influence their leadership style and interactions with others.

Psychoanalytic theory offers insights into the unconscious dynamics that can play out within organizations, such as projection, transference, and resistance. By bringing these dynamics to light, leadership development can move beyond simplistic solutions to address the root causes of organizational challenges. Leaders learn to navigate the complex emotional landscapes of their teams, fostering environments where psychological safety, trust, and authenticity flourish.

The focus on emotional health and well-being presented by theorists like Manfred Kets de Vries underscores the importance of addressing the whole person in leadership development. This holistic approach not only enhances individual leader effectiveness but also contributes to a more positive organizational culture, where mental health is prioritized, and employees feel supported and valued.

The developmental aspect of leadership, as highlighted by Erik Erikson's stages of psychosocial development, enriches leadership development models by framing leadership growth as a lifelong journey. This perspective encourages leaders to continually engage in self-reflection and personal growth, adapting their leadership approach as they navigate different life stages and challenges.

Incorporating psychoanalytic concepts into leadership development also emphasizes the importance of empathy, emotional intelligence, and the capacity for deep human connection. These qualities are increasingly recognized as critical components of effective leadership in today's complex and rapidly changing world. By fostering an understanding of the unconscious motivations that drive behavior, leaders can better connect with their teams, inspire loyalty and engagement, and lead with compassion and wisdom.

The integration of psychoanalytic concepts into leadership development models offers a profound shift in how leadership effectiveness is understood and cultivated. This approach adds depth and complexity to traditional models, equipping leaders with the tools to navigate the psychological dimensions of leadership and organizational life. By embracing this enriched perspective, leaders can develop the self-awareness, emotional intelligence, and psychological insight necessary to lead with authenticity and impact in the 21st century.

The insights drawn from psychoanalytic concepts hold transformational potential for leaders, particularly in terms of fostering authenticity, enhancing emotional intelligence, and adopting a nuanced approach to power and group dynamics. This depth of understanding offers a profound shift in how leaders perceive themselves and their interactions within the organizational milieu, paving the way for more effective, empathetic, and insightful leadership.

Authenticity emerges as a cornerstone of effective leadership when psychoanalytic insights are applied. By engaging in introspective practices and confronting unconscious biases and motivations, leaders can attain a clearer sense of their true selves. This process of self-discovery enables leaders to act in ways that are consistent with their values and beliefs, enhancing their credibility and fostering trust among followers. Authentic leaders are seen as genuine and reliable, qualities that inspire loyalty and drive collective effort toward shared goals.

Emotional intelligence is significantly deepened through an understanding of psychoanalytic principles. Leaders become adept at recognizing and managing their own emotions as well as tuning into the emotions of others. This emotional attunement allows for more compassionate, empathetic leadership, where the emotional needs of team members are acknowledged and addressed. Emotional intelligence also facilitates conflict resolution and strengthens team cohesion, as leaders are better equipped to navigate the emotional undercurrents of their organizations and mediate interpersonal dynamics constructively.

A nuanced approach to power and group dynamics is another critical area where psychoanalytic insights offer transformational potential. By understanding the psychological underpinnings of power relations and the unconscious factors that influence group behavior, leaders can wield power more responsibly and ethically. They learn to balance assertiveness with empathy, using their influence to empower others rather than dominate. Furthermore, insights into group dynamics enable leaders to foster a culture of collaboration and psychological safety, where team members feel valued and motivated to contribute their best work.

Leaders who embrace these psychoanalytic insights also become adept at managing the complexities of organizational life, including navigating change, addressing resistance, and cultivating innovation. They understand that leadership is not just about strategic decision-making but also about fostering human connections and nurturing a healthy organizational culture.

The application of psychoanalytic concepts in leadership development has the potential to profoundly transform leaders. By achieving greater authenticity, enhancing emotional intelligence, and adopting a more nuanced approach to power and group dynamics, leaders can create more inclusive, resilient, and dynamic organizations. These insights not only elevate the leader's personal growth and effectiveness but also contribute to the overall health and success of the organization, demonstrating the indelible link between psychological insight and leadership excellence.

**Integrating Insights into Executive Coaching**

Integrating insights from psychoanalytic concepts into executive coaching plays a critical role in facilitating leaders' engagement with the deeper aspects of their personality, supporting them in navigating their unconscious motivations and behaviors. This approach enriches the coaching process, offering leaders a unique opportunity to explore the underpinnings of their leadership style and the impact it has on their effectiveness and organizational culture.

Executive coaching becomes a transformative journey where leaders are encouraged to delve into their inner world, uncovering and understanding the unconscious factors that influence their thoughts, feelings, and actions. This exploration can reveal hidden strengths and previously unacknowledged challenges, providing a more comprehensive understanding of the self. Coaches skilled in psychoanalytic concepts can guide leaders through this introspective process, helping them to make connections between their personal history and their current leadership approach.

Through this deep engagement, leaders learn to recognize how their unconscious biases, defenses, and relational patterns play out in the workplace. They become more mindful of their impact on others, leading to improved interpersonal relationships and team dynamics. Executive coaching offers a safe and confidential space for leaders to reflect on their experiences, receive feedback, and experiment with new behaviors. This supportive environment is crucial for leaders to take risks in exploring their vulnerabilities and experimenting with changes in their leadership style.

Coaching focusing on psychoanalytic insights empowers leaders to address their emotional health and well-being directly. It acknowledges the emotional labor of leadership and the importance of managing one's emotional resources. Coaches can help leaders develop strategies for emotional regulation, resilience, and self-care, which are essential for sustaining their performance and avoiding burnout.

Incorporating psychoanalytic concepts into executive coaching also enhances leaders' capacity for empathy and emotional intelligence. By gaining insight into their own emotional landscape, leaders are better equipped to understand and respond to the emotions of others, fostering a more empathetic and cohesive organizational culture.

The integration of psychoanalytic insights into executive coaching offers leaders a profound avenue for personal and professional growth. It challenges them to go beyond surface-level solutions and to confront the deeper psychological aspects of leadership. This process not only benefits the individual leader but also has a ripple effect, positively impacting their teams and the broader organization. By fostering leaders who are self-aware, emotionally intelligent, and psychologically healthy, organizations can cultivate a leadership style that is adaptive, ethical, and effective, driving success in an ever-changing business environment. The value of coaches possessing a deep understanding of psychoanalytic theory cannot be overstated when it comes to guiding leaders through the challenging yet rewarding process of self-discovery and development. Such knowledge equips coaches with the tools necessary to delve beneath the surface of observable behaviors and competencies, reaching the often-unexplored territories of the unconscious mind where foundational aspects of personality, motivation, and behavior are rooted.

Coaches with expertise in psychoanalytic theory are adept at recognizing and interpreting the subtle cues and patterns that signal underlying psychological dynamics. They can identify the manifestations of unconscious processes such as transference, resistance, and projection within the coaching relationship and the broader context of the leader's professional interactions. This ability allows coaches to facilitate discussions that encourage leaders to reflect on their internal experiences and how these influence their leadership style and relationships with others.

Such coaches provide a safe and supportive environment where leaders can confront their vulnerabilities, fears, and unresolved conflicts. By gently challenging leaders to examine the psychological underpinnings of their actions and decisions, coaches foster a space for profound insight and transformation. This process of exploration and reflection can be intense and sometimes uncomfortable, requiring a coach who is not only knowledgeable but also compassionate and patient.

Coaches with a grounding in psychoanalytic theory can help leaders integrate their newfound insights into practical leadership strategies. This integration is crucial for ensuring that the self-awareness gained through the coaching process translates into tangible changes in behavior and leadership practice. Coaches can guide leaders in developing emotionally intelligent approaches to communication, decision-making, and conflict resolution, enhancing their effectiveness and impact.

The journey of self-discovery and development facilitated by such coaches is profoundly rewarding. Leaders emerge from the process with a clearer sense of self, a deeper understanding of their impact on others, and an enhanced ability to navigate the complexities of organizational life with empathy and authenticity. The benefits extend beyond the individual leader, influencing the broader organizational culture and contributing to a more emotionally intelligent, resilient, and effective leadership cadre. The role of coaches versed in psychoanalytic theory is indispensable in unlocking the full potential of leaders. Through their guidance, leaders can embark on a transformative journey that not only elevates their personal and professional growth but also fosters healthier, more dynamic organizations.

**Developing Authentic and Emotionally Intelligent Leaders**

The integration of psychoanalytic insights into leadership development emerges as not just beneficial but essential for cultivating leaders who are both effective and authentically emotionally intelligent. This approach delves deep into the core of what it means to lead, grounding leadership effectiveness in self-awareness, empathy, and the capacity for nuanced emotional navigation. Authentic and emotionally intelligent leaders, shaped by an understanding of their own psychological underpinnings, stand out for their ability to foster positive organizational cultures, inspire their teams, and adeptly navigate the intricacies of modern organizational life.

Authenticity in leadership is born out of a profound journey of self-discovery. Psychoanalytic insights prompt leaders to confront and understand their deepest motivations, fears, and desires, allowing them to lead from a place of genuine self-knowledge. This authenticity breeds trust and credibility, creating a strong foundation for leader-follower relationships. Leaders who are true to themselves can more easily align their actions with their values, demonstrating integrity that inspires confidence and loyalty in their teams.

Emotional intelligence is equally critical to leadership effectiveness, encompassing the ability to recognize, understand, and manage one's own emotions, as well as to empathize with others. Psychoanalytic concepts enrich emotional intelligence by providing leaders with the tools to explore the subconscious drivers of their emotional responses. This exploration fosters a heightened capacity for emotional regulation, enabling leaders to respond to challenges with composure and to communicate with sensitivity to the emotional states of others. Emotionally intelligent leaders are adept at creating environments where open communication, mutual respect, and emotional support flourish, contributing to team cohesion and collective resilience.

Leaders who are both authentic and emotionally intelligent are uniquely positioned to create positive organizational cultures. They embody and propagate values of transparency, integrity, and inclusivity, setting the tone for an organizational climate where every member feels valued and understood. Such leaders are also skilled at recognizing and nurturing the emotional and psychological well-being of their teams, understanding that the health of the organization is deeply connected to the health of its people.

In the face of the complexities of modern organizational life, including rapid change, diversity of workforces, and the need for innovation, authentic and emotionally intelligent leaders are indispensable. Their depth of self-understanding and emotional acuity enables them to navigate these challenges with agility and grace. They can effectively lead their organizations through transitions, manage conflict with empathy and fairness, and drive innovation by fostering a culture of psychological safety that encourages risk-taking and creativity.

The integration of psychoanalytic insights into leadership development is crucial for fostering leaders who embody authenticity and emotional intelligence. Such leaders not only elevate their own effectiveness but also enhance the collective well-being and success of their organizations. They inspire their teams, cultivate positive cultures, and navigate the complexities of organizational life with insight and compassion, marking a paradigm shift towards more humane and impactful leadership.

**Encouragement for Future Exploration**

Encouragement for future exploration into the depths of psychoanalytic theory and its application to leadership is not just a recommendation but a call to action for executive coaches, leaders, and scholars alike. This exploration represents a profound journey into understanding the human psyche and its implications for leadership effectiveness, organizational health, and personal growth. By delving into psychoanalytic concepts, individuals can uncover rich insights into the motivations, fears, and desires that drive behavior, both in themselves and others.

For executive coaches, this journey offers a toolkit for facilitating deeper change in their clients, enabling them to address not just the symptoms but the root causes of leadership challenges. Leaders, on their part, stand to gain a more nuanced understanding of their own leadership style and how it impacts their relationships and organizational culture. Scholars can contribute to this field by critically examining and expanding upon psychoanalytic theories, exploring new applications and integrations that reflect the complexities of modern organizational life.

Adopting an open-minded and reflective approach to integrating psychoanalytic insights into leadership development is essential. It requires a willingness to engage with complex and sometimes uncomfortable truths about oneself and the courage to question and adapt one's leadership practices accordingly. This process is not a one-time effort but an ongoing journey of learning and adaptation, marked by continuous self-reflection, feedback, and personal development.

The value of this exploratory journey lies not only in the immediate improvements to leadership effectiveness and organizational culture but also in the long-term benefits to leaders' personal well-being and their ability to foster healthy, resilient teams. Psychoanalytic theory provides a lens through which the intricate tapestry of human behavior in organizational contexts can be understood and navigated with greater empathy and insight.

Readers are encouraged to embrace the exploration of psychoanalytic theory as a vital component of their leadership development arsenal. Whether through formal education, self-study, or engaging in psychoanalytically informed coaching and therapy, the pursuit of these insights promises to enrich one's understanding of leadership in profound ways. In doing so, individuals can contribute to a shift towards more emotionally intelligent, psychologically aware, and, ultimately, more effective leadership practices that can meet the challenges of the 21st century with compassion, resilience, and wisdom.

**The Call to Action**

Leadership development professionals and organizations are encouraged to embrace psychoanalytic approaches as essential pathways to fostering deeper, more meaningful growth in leaders. This call to action recognizes the transformative power of psychoanalytic principles in addressing the multifaceted challenges of contemporary leadership. By integrating these approaches, leadership development can move beyond surface-level skill enhancement, reaching into the core of what drives, motivates, and sometimes hinders leaders in their roles.

Psychoanalytic approaches offer profound insights into the unconscious elements of leadership, providing leaders with the tools to understand and navigate their internal landscapes. This understanding is crucial in today's complex organizational environments, where leaders are expected to manage rapid change, resolve conflicts effectively, and maintain the psychological well-being of themselves and their teams. Psychoanalytic principles shed light on the underlying dynamics of these challenges, offering nuanced perspectives that can lead to more sustainable solutions.

In managing change, psychoanalytic approaches help leaders to recognize and address the emotional and psychological resistances that can emerge, both within themselves and among their team members. By understanding the roots of these resistances, leaders can guide their organizations through transitions with empathy and insight, reducing anxiety and fostering a culture of adaptability and resilience. Resolving conflict also benefits from a psychoanalytic lens, as it allows leaders to discern the deeper issues and emotions at play. This depth of understanding facilitates more empathetic and effective conflict resolution strategies, transforming potential divisions into opportunities for growth and deeper connection within teams.

The psychological well-being of leaders and their teams stands at the forefront of psychoanalytic approaches to leadership development. Recognizing the emotional labor involved in leadership, these approaches advocate for practices that support mental health, encourage reflective self-examination, and foster emotional intelligence. By prioritizing psychological well-being, organizations can cultivate a leadership style that is not only effective but also sustainable, enhancing the overall health of the organizational culture.

The potential for psychoanalytic principles to enrich leadership development is immense. Leadership development professionals and organizations are urged to incorporate these principles into their programs, creating spaces for leaders to explore and grow. This exploration is not only about becoming better managers or decision-makers but about evolving as individuals who can lead with authenticity, compassion, and a deep understanding of the human experience.

The integration of psychoanalytic approaches into leadership development represents a forward-thinking strategy capable of addressing the complexities of contemporary leadership. By fostering deeper, more meaningful growth in leaders, organizations can navigate the challenges of change, conflict, and well-being with greater agility and insight, setting the stage for a future where leadership is rooted in psychological depth and emotional intelligence.

**Looking Forward**

As we look to the future, the field of leadership development stands on the brink of a transformative shift, with the integration of psychoanalytic principles and leadership practice poised to play a pivotal role. This evolution reflects a growing recognition of the complexity of leadership in the modern world—a role that demands not only strategic acumen and operational expertise but also a deep understanding of human behavior, motivation, and emotional dynamics. The challenges faced by today's leaders, from navigating organizational change to fostering inclusive and resilient cultures, require insights that only a psychoanalytic approach can provide.

Anticipating future trends, we can expect to see an increased emphasis on the psychological and emotional aspects of leadership. This will likely manifest in more holistic leadership development programs that incorporate psychoanalysis not as an adjunct but as a foundational component. These programs will aim to cultivate leaders who are self-aware, emotionally intelligent, and adept at managing the unconscious dynamics that influence organizational life. As research continues to underscore the link between leader well-being and organizational health, the focus on psychological insight and emotional health will become even more pronounced.

The application of psychoanalytic principles in leadership is likely to expand beyond individual development to encompass team and organizational dynamics. Understanding the unconscious processes that underpin group behavior can provide leaders with the tools to create more cohesive, adaptive, and innovative teams. This perspective will be particularly valuable in addressing the challenges of remote and hybrid work environments, where the nuances of communication and relationship-building demand a high degree of emotional and psychological sophistication.

Technology will also play a role in shaping the future integration of psychoanalysis and leadership practice. Digital platforms and tools may emerge to support leaders in their journey of self-discovery and development, offering new ways to access psychoanalytic insights and apply them in real-time. These technological advancements, combined with traditional coaching and development methods, will provide leaders with a rich array of resources to support their growth.

The evolving field of leadership development will also see a greater emphasis on diversity, equity, and inclusion, with psychoanalytic principles offering a powerful lens through which to understand and address the unconscious biases and structural inequities that impact organizational life. By exploring the deeper psychological roots of these issues, leaders can develop more effective strategies for creating inclusive cultures that value and harness the strengths of all members.

Looking forward, the integration of psychoanalysis and leadership practice promises to enrich the field of leadership development in profound ways. By embracing the complexities of human psychology, future leadership models will not only enhance the effectiveness and well-being of leaders but also contribute to the creation of more humane, resilient, and adaptive organizations. As we navigate the uncertainties of the future, the insights offered by psychoanalytic principles will be indispensable in guiding leaders toward a vision of organizational excellence that is rooted in psychological depth, emotional intelligence, and a deep commitment to the well-being of all.

The growing recognition of the importance of psychological depth and emotional health in leadership heralds an optimistic future for the field of leadership development. This recognition is ushering in a new era where the emotional and psychological well-being of leaders is not just an afterthought but a central component of leadership development programs worldwide. As this understanding deepens, we can anticipate a future where leadership is synonymous with emotional intelligence, self-awareness, and psychological insight.

This shift reflects a broader societal acknowledgment of the complexities of human behavior and the critical role emotions play in our professional lives. The challenges of the 21st century, characterized by rapid technological advancements, global interconnectedness, and significant social and environmental issues, require leaders who can navigate these complexities with empathy, resilience, and an in-depth understanding of human motivation. The future of leadership development lies in preparing leaders not just to manage or direct but to inspire, connect, and transform.

Envisioning this future, we see leadership development programs that are rigorously designed to integrate psychoanalytic insights, providing leaders with the tools to explore their unconscious motivations, resolve internal conflicts, and understand the emotional dynamics of their teams. These programs will prioritize reflective practices, encourage vulnerability, and foster a culture of continuous personal and professional growth.

The emphasis on psychological depth and emotional health will lead to the creation of more supportive organizational cultures. Leaders who have navigated their own journey of self-discovery and development are better equipped to create environments where empathy, psychological safety, and mutual respect are paramount. In such cultures, the full potential of individuals and teams can be realized, leading to innovation, productivity, and a strong sense of community and purpose.

The integration of these elements into leadership development also promises to redefine the concept of success within organizations. Success will no longer be measured solely by financial outcomes but by the well-being of employees, the strength of interpersonal relationships, and the positive impact on society. This holistic approach to leadership development will attract a new generation of leaders committed to ethical practices, sustainability, and the creation of value for all stakeholders.

As we look to the future, there is ample reason for optimism. The growing recognition of the importance of psychological depth and emotional health in leadership is a transformative force, one that promises to shape a new paradigm of leadership development. In this future, leaders are not only effective in achieving their goals but are also compassionate, self-aware individuals who inspire those around them to reach their highest potential. This vision of leadership, grounded in emotional and psychological health, holds the promise of a more humane, resilient, and fulfilling professional world.

**Final Reflection**

As we conclude this exploration into the transformative power of psychoanalytic approaches to leadership development, it's clear that engaging with the unconscious realms of our minds offers far more than a mere enhancement to traditional leadership skills. This journey has illuminated the profound impact that such engagement can have not only on leadership effectiveness but also on personal fulfillment and the cultivation of a meaningful professional life. The central message of this book—that delving into the unconscious is a vital pathway to enriched leadership and a more fulfilling existence—resonates with a call to embrace the complexity and depth of our human experience.

Psychoanalytic approaches provide a unique lens through which we can view the challenges and opportunities of leadership. By encouraging leaders to confront and integrate their unconscious motivations, fears, and desires, these approaches offer a route to a more authentic and emotionally intelligent form of leadership.

This authenticity and emotional intelligence are critical in today's fast-paced and interconnected world, where leaders are expected to navigate complex organizational dynamics, foster inclusive cultures, and lead with compassion and empathy.

The journey into the unconscious is not always easy. It requires courage, vulnerability, and a willingness to face aspects of ourselves that we may prefer to leave unexamined. Yet, the rewards of this journey are immense. Leaders who undertake this exploration can achieve a deeper understanding of themselves and their impact on others, leading to more meaningful connections, enhanced decision-making, and the ability to inspire and motivate with genuine insight and empathy. Furthermore, the integration of psychoanalytic principles into leadership development has the potential to transform not only individual leaders but also the organizations they lead. By fostering leaders who are aware of the psychological underpinnings of their actions, organizations can create environments where trust, creativity, and collaboration flourish. This transformation can lead to healthier organizational cultures, where the well-being of employees is prioritized, and where leadership is characterized by a commitment to ethical principles and the greater good.

In reflecting on the transformative power of psychoanalytic approaches to leadership development, it becomes evident that the true measure of leadership success extends beyond achievements and accolades. Success also lies in the journey of personal growth, in the cultivation of relationships based on mutual respect and understanding, and in the contribution to creating organizations that are not only effective but also nurturing and inclusive.

This book has sought to underscore the invaluable role of engaging with the unconscious in achieving these outcomes. As we move forward, the hope is that leaders, coaches, and scholars alike will continue to explore the depths of psychoanalytic theory and its application to leadership. In doing so, they will not only enhance their capacity for effective leadership but also embark on a path to a more fulfilling personal and professional life—a journey that holds the promise of transformation, not just for themselves but for the world they seek to lead.